CONCLUSIONS OF A
PARAPSYCHOLOGIST

CONCLUSIONS OF A PARAPSYCHOLOGIST

What Paranormal Phenomena Tell Us

MICHAEL LEWIS

BALBOA.
PRESS

A DIVISION OF HAY HOUSE

Balboa Press books may be ordered through booksellers or by contacting:

Balboa Press
A Division of Hay House
1663 Liberty Drive
Bloomington, IN 47403
www.balboapress.com
1-(877) 407-4847

ISBN: 978-1-4525-7208-6 (sc)
ISBN: 978-1-4525-7209-3 (e)

Library of Congress Control Number: 2013906403

Printed in the United States of America.

Balboa Press rev. date: 06/26/2013

TABLE OF CONTENTS

INTRODUCTION

I have long felt that after so many years of investigating the paranormal, it is about time that someone presented his findings, their implications, and any legitimate conclusions in a concise, readable, non-technical format for the general public. So many investigators are content to write accounts of ghostly happenings which leave the reader to draw his own conclusions. Too many researchers like to assume a scientific stance in order to give themselves a veneer of respectability, but in doing so preclude themselves from coming to any conclusion outside the current scientific paradigm. This is a catch-22 situation, as Science does not permit its followers to stray from the straight and narrow, in case they discover anything which might disturb the carefully constructed world. Science of course likes to give its followers pride of place in today's world, like the priests of former times.

Having been involved with the paranormal since early childhood, I have finally come to the conclusion that there is a whole new world out there with momentous implications for Mankind. If scientific method, logic and reasoning are strictly applied to the mass of data, coupled with personal experience, then it becomes only too apparent that the current world view is woefully inadequate, and we behave like ostriches with our heads buried in the sands.

And what of UFOs? The weight of evidence goes back to the beginnings of recorded history, but because UFOs do not fit in with the accepted scientific viewpoint, they are totally ignored! If the man in the street glances up and sees an airliner coming into land at Heathrow, this is perfectly acceptable, but if he sees a classic flying disc, then he is condemned as a poor observer not to mention his mental ability being called into question. In this respect, life is a lottery: if you happen to see an airliner while walking down the street, you win, but if you see a flying disc, you lose. You have no control over what you happen to see in the sky, but Science either praises you or condemns you! This is the antithesis of pure Science, whose aims should be to carefully investigate everything to increase our knowledge of the world and how it works. Instead, the followers of Science predetermine what can and cannot be studied. Their predecessors, the priests of the established religions, did exactly the same thing at the Council of Nicaea with the same aim, to set themselves up in authority over their fellow men!

Against this background, is it any wonder that paranormal studies have failed to gain a foothold? The man in the street is forbidden by his religion to "dabble in the occult", and if he chooses the scientific path, he is told that because psychic phenomena cannot be measured by scientific means, there is no evidence for them and therefore they do not exist! Anyone having discernment will see the falseness of that argument, but the man in the street will take the view that Science must always be right. It is time that the man in the street woke up, and it is not my intention to brainwash but merely to inspire him to think for himself and choose his own path. Beware of those who try to lead you into their own rigid thought paths, listen to all viewpoints, accept none, study everything, follow your own spiritual path, and then you will realise how fundamentally different things really are from the generally accepted scientific and religious beliefs. Think how political and religious systems have always sought to repress Freethinkers and Radicals. We now have an unprecedented opportunity with the freedoms we enjoy in the 21st century to move forward and expand our understanding beyond the current restricted confines—let us grasp it with both hands!

waste of time. I recall being handed a photograph showing the battlefield at Culloden Moor on which the body of a dead soldier could be seen among the heather. Eagerly scanning the photograph, all I could see was the heather. In exasperation, the owner of the photograph pointed out the body, but I still couldn't see it! The photograph was snatched back by its owner who announced her intention of submitting it to "a proper expert"!! No further mention was made of this photograph, so I assume that the owner did indeed refer it to a proper expert who would have lectured her on how the human brain is adept at discerning recognisable shapes out of random images. But even so, there were occasions when I was obliged to point out certain shortcomings and this was not always appreciated.

I am often asked whether I have seen a ghost. So far the tally is two. The first occasion was during the summer of 1999 when Leicester investigator Terry Hewitt had arranged a small private investigation at the Talbot public house in Belgrave, very close to the famous Belgrave Hall. The haunting of this pub came to our attention as a result of a Psychic Day organised by ASSAP at Belgrave Hall, when the curator was told by the then pub landlady that his building was not the only one with a ghost (it is interesting to note that stories of hauntings at the two other pubs in the immediate vicinity also came to light as a result of the publicity at Belgrave Hall). I had taken part in several vigils at the pub, usually with good results, but on this occasion nothing remotely paranormal had been experienced. At 3.00.a.m we had watched a vixen and her two foxcubs nosing around the tree outside the pub, until a car had caused them to scuttle back under the gate of Belgrave Hall opposite. Soon afterwards, we posed for a group photo.

It began to get light as we prepared for the final watch, resigned to a very quiet vigil. I must explain that The Talbot has two bars, the lounge and the saloon, which are at right angles to each other. Leading off the saloon bar at the opposite end was (*(because it no longer serves this function)* a small room with gaming machines. Both bars have separate entrance lobbies, that to the saloon bar being in the corner closest to the right angle. The barman can see customers at both bars by standing behind the counter at the right angle. I was standing in the right angle, with the saloon bar on my right. Terry was upstairs changing the tapes on his video camera, the other two investigators were doing the same in the lounge bar. From my position I had a clear view of the saloon bar, and also along behind the bar to the rear lobby area through the open door at the end of the counter. From this lobby stairs lead to the upper floor, although they face away from the bar. The bar lights were on and early morning sunshine provided clear illumination. Suddenly I saw the figure of a man pass across the doorway at the end of the counter, directly in my line of vision. This surprised me, as Terry could be heard upstairs and the other two investigators were talking in the lounge bar. Anticipating that the man would go through the door in front of him into the saloon bar, I transferred my gaze to the bar side of the door (which was open). Sure enough, as large as life and bold as brass, he walked across the bar and stood by the front entrance lobby door. We stared at each other. Each seemed to be thinking "What are you doing here?" Annoyance came over me, as I assumed he must be the pub cleaner and that meant an early end to a fruitless vigil. He then turned and walked back across the bar. My training kicked in, and I observed him closely, as well as I might, being no more than six feet away!

The man was tall and thin, with a duffle or anorak coat and dark trousers. His gait rolled slightly, and he was in no hurry. The coat was rather large and hung off him, as did the hood attached to the coat. He walked into what was then the Pool Room next to the saloon bar, and out of sight. Had he turned left to retrace his steps, he would have literally bumped into Terry Hewitt who was descending the stairs at that moment. Realising that I had the keys to the pub in my pocket and was responsible for the security of the building, I decided I had to challenge him, hoping not to make too much a fool of myself with what I had every reason to believe was a member of the pub's staff. By this time Terry was at the foot of the stairs and I told him there was a man in the Pool Room. "That's the Ghost!" he exclaimed, and so confident was I that it was a mortal man I had seen, I responded "Well, that would be the biggest turn up for the book there's ever been!". We entered the Pool Room and immediately saw that it was quite empty. For me, it was a defining moment (perhaps *the* defining moment, who knows?) in my life. I then knew what a lottery winner must feel like. The elation I felt was beyond words, matched by Terry's chagrin at missing the apparition by mere seconds, and the astonishment of my two colleagues at what had happened just outside the line of their vision. By correlation with numerous other sightings of apparitions in the pub, we deduced that I had seen the ghost of a pub regular from the nineteen sixties who frequented the saloon bar in death as well as life, on one occasion going up to the bar, presenting one shilling and threepence and asking for a half of mild (beer)!

If he had done this to me, I think I would have spotted he was a ghost!! It was decided it might be worthwhile to see if this sighting could be replicated, the theory being that the time (4.29.a.m. BST) might have some significance. Another vigil was hastily arranged, which unfortunately I was unable to attend due to illness. Word had got round, and the pub was packed with ASSAP's finest. As the witching hour approached, nobody wanted to be anywhere but the saloon bar, and the comment was made that if the ghost had wanted to appear, there wouldn't have been any room for it, not to mention the risk of being blinded by a barrage of blue camera flashes!!

My second ghost sighting was in more mundane circumstances, and not, strangely enough, on a vigil. The year was 2008, and I had spent a busy day at home in Barnet. My wife was away visiting friends, and I decided that I did not want to cook, so popped out to the nearest restaurant, about 200 yards away in Barnet High Street. To reach this from my house, I had to walk for a short stretch down St Albans Road past the site of the old market. This was awaiting redevelopment and was surrounded by boarding, with a padlocked wire meshed entrance gate. This is a busy main road, with a fair number of pedestrians at most times. It gives access to the High Street and I must have passed by the market thousands of times in the thirty years I have lived in Barnet.

There are many ghost stories told about Barnet, an old coaching town on the A1 from London to York, but none relating to St Albans Road and the market. In fact St Albans Road is of relatively recent construction (eighteenth century) and a recent archaeological dig revealed nothing of interest beneath the market. The site is to the west of the mediaeval town centre and had been used as land for orchards until Victorian times. The old market was an unsightly collection of rusting early twentieth century ironwork, overdue for replacement. The only other pedestrians about in the early evening were two gentlemen who alighted from a 384 bus, and a family group emerging from the car park in Stapylton Road. My mind was still racing with thoughts from a busy day and I was not paying any attention to my surroundings, other than avoiding other pedestrians. Not the best of conditions for observing apparitions!

As I passed the market gates, I suddenly became aware of a tall, stooped man in a light raincoat carrying a small cloth bag with two cloth handles who appeared to be coming from the market entrance. The only reason I took any notice of him was that he was leaning across my shoulder as if he was in a hurry and wanted to pass in front of me. I reacted automatically and stepped to one side to let him pass. Still deep in thought I paid such scant attention that I have only a brief recollection of him passing me. Suddenly I was jolted out of my reverie by the realisation that he was no longer in sight! I looked round, and observed the family walking some distance behind me, and the two bus passengers who had crossed the road and did not appear to be making for the High Street. Puzzled I hastened to the junction with a small cul de sac a few yards ahead, thinking that he must have slipped down there. It was completely empty, and I realised that although I had paid very little attention to the man, he had vanished without trace!

Most authors leave their readers in suspense at the end of the ghostly encounter they are relating. In doing so they ensure that little if anything is learned about the unseen world, and valuable data is disregarded as anecdotal. Accounts of paranormal encounters may by themselves be no more than pieces of a jigsaw puzzle, but there is much to be learned when we try to put the puzzle together and make some sense out the pieces. To begin with the apparition at The Talbot, the first obvious point is that contrary to the assertions of sceptics, I did not conjure up a picture of the ghost I was expecting to see. As any seasoned ASSAP investigator will tell you, the last thing you are expecting to see is a ghost. I had the descriptions of several ghosts, but not of the one I actually saw. Furthermore, it was so real that despite being on the lookout for ghosts, it never occurred to me that I had finally met one!

This illustrates how the human mind will rationalise any image it receives, and try to fit it into the prevailing cultural paradigms. Thus many encounters with the paranormal are eventually accepted by the percipient as normal and rational, when in reality they are not. Doubtless you are wondering how it is that no photograph of The Talbot ghost exists, when I was surrounded by an impressive array of recording equipment and had a camera on the bar right next to me. The answer is simply that I did not recognise the appearance of the man as being in any way paranormal! Moreover, the saloon bar was the only part of the area under surveillance which was not covered by a video camera. Ghosthunters long ago recognised that ghosts are notoriously camera shy, and good photographs are rare. What happened at The Talbot was true to form. We can therefore safely say that the spiritual laws which govern the unseen world prevent ghosts from appearing on film. To the sceptic this is proof positive that ghosts do not exist: a classic example of drawing the wrong conclusion from the data. Another point to arise is that the best way to recognise a ghost is by its dress. In the case of The Talbot, the dress was pure nineteen sixties and corresponded with a period when a half of mild was indeed one shilling and three pence. It was the outmoded manner of dress that prompted me to challenge the apparition.

Sometimes a ghost has a particular significance for the percipient, as the Talbot ghost appeared to have for me. The time and place of its appearance meant that only I could see it: a few seconds later, or anywhere else in the pub would have exposed it to the view of other investigators. I felt at the time that it was stage managed for me, and so it proved, as I experienced a period of illness for several months thereafter, and, with my belief in the spiritual world renewed, this led to my initiation into Reiki. Thus we can conclude that appearances of apparitions can be purposeful, and imply interaction between the worlds. The apparition at Barnet market is rather more puzzling. It did not make any attempt to be seen, and seemed only concerned with making off at speed. There was no interaction with the percipient. To explain it, we must use another scientific principle— correlation with other such incidents in the street. A wealth of data is available. I recall an ASSAP Committee meeting at which the case of an apparition outside Beckenham Junction station was being discussed. The witness had related how she had seen a teenage girl in rather dated dress wandering outside a nightclub in some distress. Other pedestrians were changing direction to avoid colliding with her, so this was not a subjective experience. The witness was moved by the girl's strange appearance to look back, and thus was able to see her as she disappeared! The sceptical Committee was grudgingly forced to conclude that not everyone you might meet in the street was necessarily of this world, and I was instructed that in future if I had reason to suspect that I had encountered a ghost, I should attempt to make verbal and physical contact.

An intriguing and relevant story was related to me by a student of Professor Chris French, the tv sceptic no less, who can surely be relied upon to turn out students with a healthy disrespect for the paranormal! The lady was on her way to work in Leicester Square one morning when she was accosted by a pale, forlorn young lady who asked her "Is there any life round here?". The witness was not normally prone to stopping for vagrants on the way to work, but something about the girl's appearance caused her to take pity. She stopped and suggested that the girl followed her to a café nearby where she could get a warm drink. The girl followed her, and she recalled holding the café door open for the girl to enter. Descending the steps to the basement café, she paused at the bottom and turned, only to find the door closed and the stairway empty. Retracing her steps to the street, the witness could see no sign of the girl. Sceptics will of course say that the girl did not go through the door, but turned and ran: what could possibly be the motive? A free cup of coffee was on offer! Yet another example of what I term an apparition in the street actually happened to me, and is included in the chapter on angels. Given these encounters, I can even half believe UFO enthusiasts who claim aliens move amongst us—at the very least the data says this is feasible. So why do street apparitions appear to random passers by? What does it mean? The implications are, I think, very serious for both society and established religion. Taking the man coming out of Barnet market, I think this was an example of a lost soul carrying on with his earthly routine after death. A few years ago, shoppers of this description could be seen every Saturday in Barnet market. The man was merely following his old habits, and his only concern was that his swift exit was being obstructed by a slow moving pedestrian. In the case of the apparition at Beckenham Junction, could this have been a clubber who had unhappy associations with the nightclub, perhaps having taken drugs there with fatal results? The same might be surmised about the young girl in Leicester Square. The Church tells us that in death we are at peace with the Lord (or asleep, waiting for an Archangel to wake us up with a trumpet blast according to your religious persuasion), but as I relate in the chapter on my own Near Death Experiences, this is far from the truth. The reality, I fear, is rather more prosaic: it would appear that some souls who led a life of comforting routine lack the intellectual ability to move on to something better, which for them would be an unthinkable leap in the dark, while other souls, who died in unhappy circumstances prematurely may fail to come to terms with the fact that they are dead, and try to regain their former life ("life" in the words of the girl at Leicester Square is surely significant).

Another aspect of the paranormal which has significant implications for the parapsychologist, if only they would stop and think, is the appearance and disappearance of objects in poltergeist cases, hauntings and Spiritualist séances. "Ex nihilo nihil fit" is a sound scientific principle which guides my thinking here. Matter cannot come out of nothing (although this begs the question of how did matter get here in the first place) and solid objects cannot pass through other solid objects such as walls. Science in its purest form is knowledge of everything which exists, problems only arise when scient*ists* make pronouncements on what exists, determined by what they can explain at any given time. If you accept this point, the shortcomings of scientists are only too apparent, indeed the history of science is littered with examples of this: atom, for example, comes from the Greek, 'that which cannot be split'; when radioactivity was first demonstrated, respected physicists of the day were unable to accept this new concept. Clearly what is needed here is lateral thinking, provided it does not contravene the laws of physics (although their precise definition is under constant challenge!).

A case in point concerned a lady in Hertfordshire who was plagued with poltergeist phenomena. Money would disappear, not only in physical form from her handbag, but also electronically from her bank account. Problems would arise when she found herself in situations with no money, although she had placed adequate money in her purse before leaving the house. Nor was the bank able to produce supporting documentation for withdrawals from her account, paid cheques had been "lost".

Does this provide a possible explanation for the provenance of coins found at the scene of poltergeist disturbances? And what happens to money removed electronically—does it appear in someone else's account? Or is this another explanation for the sudden collapse of the global banking system?! Alternatively, it may be that "the other side" is able to produce anything by the power of pure thought, in which case how futile life on earth is, when we could all be in Shangri-la without working! It is true to say that if we could grasp the concepts which appear to be at the root of cases in which objects appear and disappear, our whole way of thinking would be changed, and our world view radically altered. Is this what New Agers mean by "Ascension"? At the very least, the disappearance and reappearance of objects can only be accounted for in scientific terms by the existence of other dimensions. By changing their rate of atomic vibration, objects pass into a different dimension, invisible to our eyes, and then are able to reappear somewhere else in the original dimension. This concept is at the heart of the Hadron Collider, and I am told that quantum physicists already believe in the existence of other dimensions. When this has been proved, the next step will be to find out whether there are any living organisms in other dimensions. Future funding for the Hadron Collider has not been agreed, perhaps because The Establishment does not want Pandora's box to be opened . . . .

Not all my experiences have been concerned with ghosts. I recall debating whether to participate in a fire walk which was on offer at a conference I was attending. I had read an account of Harry Price's exploits on the Brocken and felt that if it was safe for him to do, then it would surely be safe for me! Having thus gained sufficient confidence, I booked to do the fire walk, but I began to have doubts as the event approached. When the day of reckoning dawned, I have to confess that I was in a dreadful state! Matters were not helped when the organisers announced that they were not going to do the fire walk themselves, and it was off you go! I had realised when I booked it that this was not going to be a charity type fire walk when the outside top of the glowing charcoal is at a relatively low temperature, and the trick is simply not to stand still. This was for real! I gazed fearfully at the long carpet of orange and red embers. Almost immediately a lady strode forth, others followed, and I felt obliged to follow suit. It certainly was another defining moment in my life! I strode forth—I cannot say confidently—and arrived at the other side with glowing embers falling from my feet. On the second run I waited until the embers had been rekindled, to avoid any suggestion that I had waited for them to cool down! I deliberately trod hard on a red ember, and felt a slight twinge. Others told me that they had done the same, and had also felt a slight twinge. I also observed that small parts of the glowing embers tended to stick to one's feet, and fall off as the runner slowed down in the grass. As far as I was concerned, I had disproved, through personal experience, the oft quoted theory that one did not come into contact with the glowing embers for long enough for the heat to damage the foot. If this were indeed so, then the glowing embers which stuck in some numbers to the feet of the runners would have caused burns.

When I hit the employment trail in the mid sixties there was no question of finding any employment which would fit in with my interest in the paranormal. This was long before the New Age movement, and the only way of investigating ghosts was to join the Society for Psychical Research. In these circumstances, I felt that a career in the Church would be an acceptable compromise, and so I joined the Church of England as a clerical officer in the Houses Department at the Church Commissioners for England, at a starting salary of £777! Unlike today, it was the custom to pursue a career within the same organisation, and I stayed there for 38 years until I had the wherewithal to set up on my own as a parapsychologist. Initially I was plagued by various health problems, one of which led to my near demise (and resulted in a series of NDEs which are described in another chapter). Before leaving full time employment, I had trained with Doreen Virtue at Glastonbury as an AngelTherapist™. I also had Reiki 2 under my belt, following a period of illness during which I was advised to learn Reiki myself as it was having a beneficial effect. After becoming an AngelTherapist™ it was but a natural progression to learn Angelic Reiki which I found a more powerful therapy. I also took up crystal healing after encountering the church of Shambhala, which has a headquarters in the States and a small monastery in Glastonbury. Subsequently I acquired an impressive array of their healing tools, including a magnificent pyramid!

CHAPTER 2

A WALK WITH THE ANGELS

I was brought up under the Church of England and at that time it was usual to be taught about angels as winged creatures. Most people believed in the literal truth of the Bible, although even as early as the 1960s a tendency to explain Biblical events in rational, scientific terms was already creeping in. But in the last decade of the 20th century, there was an explosion of interest in Angels. A little bemused by this, I decided to attend an Angel event organised by Diana Cooper. I was impressed by the enthusiasm of the large throng, and my interest grew to the extent that I attended workshops by both Diana and Doreen Virtue. I recall one memorable event when we were asked to listen for the voice of an angel. To my surprise I heard the name Jophiel, which I struggled to spell. I was somewhat overawed to be informed, in reverential tones, that he was the Archangel of wisdom. Having made the first step, I took things a stage further. Invoking Jophiel one night for help with a problem, I was astonished to experience a dream in which I was working through the problem! Gradually I learned to recognise when the angelic realm was speaking to me. The process was known as clairsentience and is the same means by which spirits and other entities communicate. I recall sitting in a deck chair one morning thinking how nice it would be to retire. Evidently someone was tuning in to my thoughts as a distinctive voice exclaimed "You won't be here in 10 years' time!" The voice sounded very real, and I interpreted this as meaning that I had work I to do which would necessitate a move.

Another example of angelic guidance took place when I was at a conference on crop circles at Devizes. I was recovering from illness at the time, and on the eve of the conference the Archangel Raphael suggested that I was now well enough to make further progress spiritually. The next morning I arrived at the conference hall bright and early. A stall advertising helicopter trips to view the circles caught my attention. I had had a lifelong aversion to flying, but thought how much I would like to see the circles from the air. Such was my fear of flying, I ruled out a flight automatically, without giving the matter a second thought. Again, someone had read my thoughts! The Archangel Michael immediately asked me why I was afraid of flying when he was there to protect me! I was nonplussed! The logic of the argument was incontrovertible. Furthermore, it dawned on me that the angels were acting in concert and if I still resisted, another angel would have a go at me and then another and another— how many angels were there! While I was deliberating, the only other person in the hall at that early hour approached me. Apologising for intruding, the lady told me that she was an AngelTherapist from the States, and she just had to tell me that I was surrounded by archangels, as she could see their light around me. I decided that the only thing to do in these circumstances was to give up before anything else happened! There and then, I went over to the helicopter stall and booked a flight the next day.

When the time came for the flight, I was feeling slightly apprehensive. I was strapped in next to the pilot, with a microphone on an open circuit for communication with the pilot and other passengers, as the noise from the twin engines precluded any conversation. The helicopter lifted off backwards at a very steep angle and at an astonishing speed. A lady in the back screamed in fright but I was determined to maintain my composure! The pilot apologised to his passengers and explained that because he was in a built-up area, Civil Aviation Authority regulations required him to take off in this alarming manner. To look down on the patchwork quilt of fields below required nerves of steel from someone who had never climbed more than three rungs on a ladder. It was almost as if I was in an altered state of consciousness. Since helicopter flights were short as well as costly, my ordeal was soon over, and the ground rushed up to meet us at a terrifying speed. Then it seemed to stop, and I realised that we had landed without so much as a bump. I sensed a host of angels cheering me. As far as I was concerned that was that, I was now willing to fly. During the flight I had taken some photos, including one which showed the pilot and the ground far below. On returning home I showed these to my wife who could only interpret them as taken in a taxi from the side of a mountain (*in Wiltshire!*). She absolutely refused to believe that I had flown! Not long afterwards the reason for all this was made clear. That autumn my son graduated at Glasgow University. Unfortunately this coincided with flooding and maintenance difficulties on the railways which made long journeys impossible due to speed restrictions and flood damage to the tracks. The only feasible way of travelling such a distance was to fly, and to the astonishment of my family that was exactly what I did. I can honestly say that I felt quite happy about flying there and back. In relating this story, I feel that I have a duty to warn others against trying this themselves! What I did to overcome my fear of flying goes against all medical advice. For someone with such a deep rooted and lifelong fear of flying, I have to say that I needed to be 100% (not just 99%) *certain* of the existence of a powerful Archangel who had promised to keep me safe. In any other circumstances such a course of action would be extremely unwise and should not be attempted, because it might jeopardise the safety of the aircraft and other passengers.

In 2005 Doreen Virtue finally fulfilled her long standing promise to run an AngelTherapy™ course in England after it had been pointed out to her that the course she had run previously in Ireland did not count, as Ireland was in reality a different country, no matter how the Americans viewed it! I booked the course as soon as it was announced, as the dollar was at a low and I feared it might rise. At the same time I booked a room in a luxury hotel in Glastonbury before Doreen had a chance to reserve the whole hotel for her retinue. Thus it was that I found myself sharing the same hotel as Doreen—an added bonus. A further bonus was that I was just one of 19 male attendees compared with 181 females!! A session spent giving angel readings to a succession of lovely young things was quite an experience in more senses than one! But I digress. Parts of the course were familiar territory for me but other parts were uncharted waters. A point of contention for me was the teaching that we had all incarnated from other realms, and that these were our true spiritual homes. I was soon to learn how true this was (see chapter on NDEs).

One memorable excursion was to Stonehenge at a very early hour on a very cold May morning. As we walked around the stones, a hare leaped up towards us out of the grass and promptly dropped down dead at our feet. Our guide, who was quite clearly not a spiritual person, exclaimed that he had never seen a hare in all the years he had been at Stonehenge. Needless to say there was much excited discussion about the meaning of this event. I believe that hares have some significance in Druidism, but in any event the death of the hare was no coincidence.

We were taught how to cut emotional chords which were holding people back in their lives. This was a new concept for me but its efficacy was dramatically illustrated when my sitter thanked me for selling her house the next day. During her sitting, I had detected a strong female attachment which she had acknowledged and asked me to remove, which I did. She explained that she had been trying to sell her house for some time without success. Her mother lived nearby and did not wish her to move out of the area. Once the cord had been cut, two people had viewed her house that very evening, and one had made an offer which she had accepted. You may wonder how I managed to do that (if you think that is a pure coincidence, why did you bother to read this?). I simply followed instructions! It brought home to me how much there is about the universe and how it works which is entirely unknown to us, but which can easily be harnessed to our advantage.

By far the most dramatic incident took place one sunny evening in my hotel room. I had just returned after the final course session of the day, and was perched on the end of my bed perusing the handouts which I had received that day. Suddenly the room was filled with a blinding white intense light. A very deep male voice sounded in my ear: "I am Metatron. You can work with me". I was so startled that I confess to falling off the edge of the bed onto the floor! Well, you would, wouldn't you?! My training kicked in, and I checked light sources within the room and outside. The yellow room light was on, but paled beside the brilliance of the white light which had vanished as suddenly as it had appeared. Outside the sunlight was still bright, and no one was in the garden taking photographs with a flash. I had been told on the course and had read in books that this is how angels sometimes appear. Like most of the phenomena that I investigate, I was confident that this would never happen to me, but now it had! If you take accounts of this nature with a pinch of salt, rest assured that they do indeed happen. It happened to me, and there is nothing like personal experience!

Perhaps the most evidential incident occurred on the last morning. We had been asked not to take photographs, except for a photo shoot at the end. Immediately the course had finished, I went around taking photographs. Something told me that I should not be taking photographs without asking for permission. I took a couple of photographs after asking permission, then it was time for a group photograph with Doreen Virtue. On leaving the hall for the last time, I viewed my photographs on the LCD display, and was horrified to see that my camera had developed a serious fault which had ruined many of the shots. On reaching my hotel room, I took a photograph in case the problem was connected with the hall. That certainly proved to be the case! The photograph taken in the hotel bedroom showed no signs of any blurring and was quite clear. The photographs I had taken without permission in the hall showed what appeared to be shafts of light to the extent that they made the photograph unrecognisable. Photographs taken with permission were recognisable, but were still affected to some extent by what looked like mist around the edges. Another spectacular demonstration that there are indeed laws in the universe of which most people are in complete ignorance.

The surprises which I experienced at Glastonbury were not confined to my Angel course. On a subsequent visit to the Glastonbury Symposium I found myself in the very well known Galatea restaurant for an evening meal. A group of ladies were seated at a table at the other end of the restaurant. Suddenly one of them left the table, walked to my table, and asked me if I would like to join them as they too were attending the symposium. I accepted the invitation and the conversation turned to the topic of the Goddess movement about which I knew very little. The next day, during the lunch break, I decided after the previous evening's conversation that I would visit the Goddess Temple for a laugh. I half expected to be thrown out but was pleasantly surprised to find a very agreeable atmosphere. In fact I quite liked the place. On leaving I went to put a one pound coin in the makeshift collection box as is my custom. The box was the usual shoebox with a slot cut in the lid. To my embarrassment it would not go in. Glancing down I observed that the slot was cut sufficiently wide to receive two-pound coins which are the largest in circulation. Taking aim more carefully, I tried to drop the coin in the centre of the slot. It still would not go in, although there was no reason for this. Fearing that the temple attendants would think I was one of the great unwashed trying to steal their collecting box, I left the coin on top of the box and made a hasty exit. Thinking this over, it dawned on me that I had not entered the temple with the best of attitudes, and the Goddess, whose existence I confess I had doubted, had declined to accept an offering which was not given with the best of intentions. Another important lesson learned! The next day after coming to terms with the existence of the Goddess, I revisited the temple and on leaving placed a one pound coin in the collection box without any difficulty, to my great relief!

Although I could never quite understand how angel card readings usually produced results meaningful to the sitter, I soon found out just how well they worked with me. The very first paid reading I performed had a dramatic start. I had taken a stall at a fair and the first card drawn provoked the response from the sitter that it related not to her, but to her friend. At this juncture the sitter's mobile phone rang, and it occurred to me that this might be the very same friend. Ending the call quickly, the sitter exclaimed "Freaky! That was the friend for whom the card was meant!" I knew neither the sitter nor her friend, nor did the friend ring more than once a week. *Yet this was the first card reading I had done outside training!* I was at a loss to explain how this could possibly have happened, and my first sitter was certainly as astonished as I was.

This incident led me to make a close study of the mechanics of angel card readings. I tried letting a third party shuffle the cards, something which most people who give card readings would be horrified at, with the same positive results. I did find, however, that when I changed my methodology, the card selected was not meaningful to the sitter, something which was normally a rare event. It was quite clear to me that chance played no part in card readings, but I was baffled as to how the angelic realm influenced the choice of cards. In this business one has to think laterally, and I eventually came to the conclusion that, once I had established my methodology, the angelic realm simply substituted the card they wished me to select for the one which my shuffling of the pack would have produced by chance. I realise that this is revolutionary thinking, but it fits in with what I was told on my NDEs (see later chapter), namely that the physical world is not as we perceive it and that we can create any illusion which we (or any other being) wish to create as seeming reality. Another pointer to this is the apports which have been well recorded by investigators of hauntings (see previous chapter).

CHAPTER 3

GHOSTS

A s I said in the introduction, this is not a collection of ghost stories. Indeed, I have already recounted my own two sightings of ghosts. Rather, I would prefer to relate individual occurrences to see what we can learn from them. Much has been written about ghosts but there has been very little discussion about what we can deduce from the phenomenon.

Stone throwing is often associated with poltergeist cases. I recall an incident which took place at the prestigious London headquarters of a well known national institution. John Spencer, who is renowned as being a very level headed and methodical parapsychologist, reported that on a vigil which we attended in the building, stones had been thrown at him. Most had hit the panelled wall of the corridor but one had struck a fellow investigator on the head. As is often the case, no harm was caused to the investigator as the stone did not strike his head with any force. A curious feature was that the stones felt hot to the touch. Now I am not a physicist but some energy was required to propel the stone through the air. Could this have been heat extracted from the atmosphere, hence the warmth in the stones? And does this explain why cold spots are sometimes found in haunted houses?

A puzzling feature of many hauntings is the movement of objects, often involving their disappearance and reappearance. How is this accomplished? The most likely explanation would seem to be that a discarnate entity has applied sufficient force to move the object in the same way as it did when in an earthly body. When objects disappear and reappear, it would seem that they pass into another dimension through the agency of a spirit which has learnt how to change the rate of vibration of the object's atoms to that of its own. Sometimes an object of great significance is moved or disappears, for example, an item of jewellery belonging to a deceased person, and it would be a fair assumption that the deceased person wished to convey their continued existence. Apports are also a great puzzle. I recall one researcher telling me that he had witnessed an apple materialise in someone's hand! Does this mean that an apple has suddenly vanished from a fruiterer's shop somewhere without anybody noticing, or has it been created? If the latter then precisely what are the mechanics? Has it been produced from basic matter in this dimension, or from matter in another dimension?

A feature of vigils which I attended at Woodchester Mansion in Gloucestershire was that female investigators invariably complained that their hair was stroked when sitting in the chapel. On the first occasion I was accused of doing this, even though I would have needed a very long arm to achieve this from where I was sitting! On future occasions I made sure I was sitting in the side room to the chapel to avoid this accusation. Since this never happened to male investigators it is to be assumed that the chapel was haunted by a lonely male spirit! But this does not explain the haunting of the bathroom of a London pub, said to be the ghost of a gay pub worker, as it was especially active when the barmaid took a shower!

Another feature of Woodchester Mansion was the tolling of a bell in the mansion's bell tower. All the investigators on one vigil heard a single toll when assembled in the drawing room. It certainly stopped the hubbub of conversation! Investigation revealed that not only was access to the bell tower blocked off for safety reasons, but the clapper of the bell was firmly tied to the bell itself. It could not have been rung so were we hearing an etheric recording?

Ghosts are notoriously shy, and the behaviour of a very old clock at the Mansion demonstrated this clearly. Before starting on a tour to get acquainted with the layout, we admired a very old pendulum clock which obviously did not go. After a lengthy tour we came upon the clock and immediately noticed that the pendulum was swinging to a noticeable degree. As we gazed at it, it slowed down and finally stopped. By careful observation during watches we concluded that when left alone it started to increase momentum gradually. This took some time, and if we checked on the movement after leaving it for a short time, the pendulum had not gained very much momentum in its arc, whereas if it was left for a full hour, then the pendulum would swing in a wider arc. It had been able to achieve a significant momentum in the first instance because all the investigators were elsewhere in the house for a reasonable period and there was no possibility of anyone observing it. Once the clock was observed to be working, the pendulum lost momentum until it had stopped.

The fact that ghosts are notoriously shy and phenomena seem to be inhibited by the presence of investigators was once again demonstrated. Now why should this be? Sceptics of course find this proof positive that ghosts do not exist, but unbiased investigators look for a reason. Given that the whole Universe follows the laws of physics which have been painstakingly mapped out by Science, it seems logical to suppose that ghosts are no exception. Either God has decreed that we must be left alone to make sense of the world by ourselves (otherwise there would be no point in incarnating to learn lessons), or, if the idea of God does not appeal, then perhaps ghosts are subject to the same physical laws as everything else, and these laws may prevent direct communication for sound, though undiscovered, scientific reasons. That said, there have of course been instances where phenomena and apparitions have occurred in the presence of investigators, but in my experience these are rare. It may perhaps be in such instances that actual physical phenomena are not occurring (and would not be captured on a camera) but the percipient *thinks* that they are real. My own sighting at The Talbot was real enough to me, but the acid test would have been to capture it on camera. Like all good ghosts, it appeared in the only part of the pub not covered by video cameras!

The question of fraud is always uppermost in the investigator's mind. Easier to resolve is the question of misinterpretation. This can be addressed by a combination of training courses and long practical experience. Inexperienced investigators will always report incidents which a more experienced investigator would attribute to natural phenomena. Again, this is manna for the sceptics who lump all kinds of investigators into one class—gullible! Worst of all are the thrill seeker type of investigator who do not take the subject very seriously. Anything they report is likely to be regarded with suspicion. The rise in popularity of TV programmes such as "Most Haunted" has caused the number of paranormal groups to mushroom, and such groups rarely have much knowledge of the issues involved in serious investigation. Whereas the type of incident depicted on TV does happen in serious investigations, it is the exception rather than the rule. Most ASSAP investigators will recall long, often cold nights spent fruitlessly in haunted locations. So how is it that TV investigations usually uncover a hive of activity? A well known medium recounts how, after touring a haunted location with a television crew, he had to admit to the producer that he wasn't picking much up. "Fine", replied the producer, "but can't you make something up?". Needless to say the medium did not last long on the programme! Most investigators have a similar story to tell of investigations covered by the media.

The question of sounds heard in buildings at night is a vexed one. All investigators are familiar with thermal noises from the structure as temperatures fall. But such noises are often very similar to those produced by ghosts. We are told—and it seems logical—that because of the difficulty in communicating between the dimensions and in order to use the least energy possible, sounds produced paranormally will usually be at the threshold of audibility. Is it not therefore possible that discarnate entities may manipulate naturally occurring energies to produce a regular pattern in order to indicate intelligent communication?

I recall a possible such incident during a vigil at Watford Central Library under the auspices of the Anglia Paranormal Investigation Society (APIS). The vigil had been requested by the library as part of a Halloween book promotion. I recall being in the main library during the early hours when I heard a series of creaks at regular intervals. The library had large wooden beams supporting the roof which would undoubtedly creak as they contracted due to the falling temperature, but would they creak at such regular intervals, unless to attract my attention? I was unable to decide, but this is the sort of question the serious investigator needs to address. (Amusingly, we were unable to investigate the room which we had determined as being the most active, as the staff on duty thought it was the cosiest room to settle down in with their coffee!).

The phenomena at the library are well attested, so what can be causing them in a nineteen thirties building on former open marshland? The answer does, I feel, teach us something about other realms which is far from the cosy picture painted by the Church or the escapist nihilism of Science. Like others on the investigation I attempted to tune into the next dimension, and like the others, I picked up mischievous children. Old maps in the library showed that the area to the east of the present High Street was once the site of Victorian slums, and the inference was that children from the dire tenements adjoining had not moved on, but still lingered in their old haunts, and were attracted by the library. This would explain why the staff not infrequently observed the main door open when no-one could be seen, and the childish antics such as the throwing of books onto the floor, which was actually observed at the start of our vigil.

From this we would deduce that slum children who often died young, lacking an education or a religious upbringing, stayed in what was to them familiar surroundings, still causing mischief. If this is the case, then cases such as this would indicate the presence of a vast unseen host around us, responsible for what we term paranormal occurrences, and, rather more worryingly, probably influencing us in ways we can only guess at. Might this be an explanation for criminal or erratic behaviour among the living?

I recall being told by a clairvoyant during a vigil at the caves under Nottingham's Broadmead Shopping Centre that we were being watched by an apprehensive band of former workers in the caves, which were at one time utilised by the dyeing industry. These lowly workers had not been paragons of virtue during their lives, and had preferred to remain in their old occupation for fear of the hell which the church had foretold awaited them. They were fearful that we might be representatives of the Church or demons who had come to take them away to Hell. If this is so, then Religion has a lot to answer for and it may explain why the Church is so anxious to dissuade its followers from any contact with the departed, lest they learn the horrible truth, as I did during the NDEs described in a later chapter!

To return to the question of fraud, it is, like the poor, ever with us. For the sceptic it provides the perfect explanation for anything which cannot be explained away by other means. Paranormal researchers are well aware that stage magicians can produce most of the phenomena which occurs in hauntings, but that does not stop them from investigating hauntings (this explains why stage magicians are traditionally hostile to the paranormal, although it has been hinted that some have disguised paranormal abilities under the magician's cloak). Quite simply, it is usually pretty easy to determine whether the percipients are stage magicians, and in any event it is blatantly obvious that the vast multitude of percipients cannot possibly all be stage magicians! Most investigators of the paranormal have encountered fraud, and often the reason is a desire to boost the hoaxer's ego and take pleasure in deceiving others. Unworthy motives, but very common behaviour among many people. Sceptics have it as an article of faith that all phenomena in council houses can be attributed to a desire for better accommodation, but I have never personally come across such a case where this was so. So many explanations which have gained acceptance among the general public are simply not supported by the evidence, and the sceptics' case is shown to be built on very shallow foundations. In general, investigators look for independent corroboration, something which the sceptics totally ignore. Cases where there is only one witness, although not without interest, cannot be relied upon as evidential unless there are correlations with other cases. To sum up by way of an analogy, there are still art collectors around, even though the existence of forgeries is well known.

The emergence of what is loosely known as the New Age Movement has forced the parapsychologist to broaden his horizons, to the good of his studies. When I started out in the late fifties, the only form of channelling was by mediums between the living and the dead, and was largely confined to Spiritualism. When strange people calling themselves experiencers and channellers came over from the United States, they were met with bewilderment by their counterparts over here! Gradually the truth dawned that we needed to widen our horizons, and that there were indeed many other dimensions as Christ himself told his followers. It became apparent that there were implications for parapsychologists in that there might be additional explanations for what had been classified, perhaps erroneously, as ghosts and that the dichotomy between UFOs and ghosts had created an artificial barrier which had prevented progress in gaining an overview of the complete picture. I am proud to say that from the outset of my interest in UFOs (described more fully in a later chapter), I took the view that because of similarities with other forms of paranormal phenomena, they were a branch of psychical research rather than being entirely divorced from it. In my view UFOs came from parallel universes rather than from distant parts of our Universe. When I joined the British Unidentified Flying Object Research Association (BUFORA) in 1971, I was a lone voice and the nuts and bolts fraternity ruled the roost, thus ensuring that British Ufology went down the wrong track for many years. Returning to the subject of ghosts however, I believe the first priority after establishing that there is a phenomenon to be investigated is to determine the category into which it falls. I recall in the old days sightings of UFOs and ghostly figures in rural Kent near the south coast. If a local paranormal group received a report of a UFO, it was simply passed on to the nearest UFO group. Conversely, if a UFO group received a report of a ghostly figure, it would be passed on to the local paranormal group! But if a report was received which contained both elements, the UFO group investigated. Looking back, correlations can be drawn between the entities seen in the vicinity of UFOs and ghostly figures not associated with UFO sightings. How a report was investigated depended on whether a UFO was seen or not. With hindsight it was apparent that there was a UFO flap going on in the area at the time, but rigid lines of demarcation prevented investigators from gaining the complete picture.

The lesson was that investigators need to adopt a much broader remit, which I am pleased to say is more often the case today. A case in point is the earthquake which struck Britain in the early hours of February 27th 2008. Minutes before the quake struck, I had gone to the kitchen of my house in North London for a drink, unable to sleep. I was astonished to observe an irregular shaped pale green light, about the size of a butterfly, flitting about in the dining room. After attempting to find a natural explanation I went to get my camera, but it had disappeared in the short time this took me. It was completely outside my experience or knowledge, but a colleague surmised that this was an earth spirit, released by the tremors from the earthquake. What is an earth spirit, you might well ask? Well, I don't know either, but it is logical to presume that there are nature spirits within the earth as well as on it, not to mention in the sea and air as well. We should collect all the pieces of the jigsaw puzzle, regardless of whether or not we can fit them into the full picture.

But to return again to the core subject of ghosts, once you have established that the phenomena under investigation may correctly be placed in that category, the data strongly suggests that discarnate entities who have failed to move on are responsible. But failed to move on to where? From my own Near Death Experiences (NDEs), the answer seems to depend on the personal beliefs (or lack of them) of each individual. This is an important question, because the answer could shed much light on the behaviour of ghosts and thereby benefit investigators. Spiritualists have their Summerland, where they dwell happily with those who have predeceased them. Christians expect St Peter to open the pearly gates where Jesus waits to embrace them (although some Protestants expect to sleep until awakened by the Archangel's trumpet blast; in my case, not coming from a tradition of Saints I was not greatly concerned by the absence of St Peter to greet me during my first NDE!). Other religions have their own traditions, and no doubt adherents encounter what they have been told to expect. Given that other dimensions into which we pass are unconstrained by the same physical laws, there would seem to be little problem in creating whatever the dying person was expecting to see. My thoughts on the implications of all this may be found in the final postscript.

The problems which concern the parapsychologist seem to stem from the large numbers of people with no firm religious beliefs, or no belief in an afterlife. In this respect it is a little galling that the likes of such sceptics as Professor Chris French, who at least are knowledgeable of the beliefs they decry, will have little problem in accepting their new circumstances after death, albeit perhaps tinged with a little regret that their entire earthly life had followed the wrong path!! Many of those who cause trouble to the current occupiers of the places familiar to them in their earthly lives either do not realise that they are dead, or feel safe and secure in familiar surroundings. Logic alone dictates that anyone with a continuing consciousness who firmly believes that death is the end will not accept that they have died and will do their best to communicate with those still in the body. The film "The Others" is a superb depiction of the reality of this! Examples to support this viewpoint abound. Whilst on a vigil at the Galleries of Justice in Nottingham (don't forget to take your chequebook as well as your camera), I was seated on a bench next to a window in one of the cells when I distinctly felt something prod me in the ribs. My whole body tingled and I gleefully recorded the first paranormal event of the night in my logbook. My clairvoyant companion saw me start and grinned. She had, she said, been watching the ghost of a young woman prisoner lying on the bed in the cell. Obviously this entity had been used to sitting on the bench to look out of the window, and resented my occupying her usual place. Eventually she had got up, walked over to the bench, and prodded me in the ribs in an attempt to dislodge me. Of course sceptics will decry this as anecdotal, but the volume of evidence over the years convinces me that ghosts do interact with us.

The late researcher Andrew Green recounted how in his youth he had visited a haunted house in Montpelier Avenue, Ealing. Some 21 persons had committed suicide by jumping off the small tower at the top of the large house (long since demolished). He told me that he had himself gone to this tower and become convinced that he could just step over the parapet onto the grass below! Fortunately his father had accompanied him and was able to restrain him. Did the ghost of the first suicide influence the other twenty suicides? Or was there another factor at work? Whatever the explanation, it is clear that chance alone could not account for so many suicides.

What is abundantly clear, in case after case, is that persons who have formed an attachment with a particular building often prefer to remain there after death. They are not necessarily earthbound, but the treadmill of work and routine holds a greater attraction for them than the prospect of a radical change of lifestyle. Conservative in life, conservative in death perhaps? Human beings seem to have a great fear of change, despite the benefits which progress can bring. In this respect I call to mind with some amusement the struggles of Henry Ford to persuade the manufacturers of horse drawn carriages in the USA to put his new horseless carriage into production. "It'll never catch on" they told him, "people prefer horses". In the end Ford was forced to set up production himself in order to get his invention off the ground! Have you ever heard of the Ford motor company?! Do you know of a manufacturer of horse drawn carriages flourishing today?! The analogy is obvious!

A case in point is The Guildhall at Cambridge. A building has existed on the site since 1200, and in mediaeval times there was a wooden bridge from the front of the building to the market hall on the site of the present open air market place. The imposing building which today dominates the market square is relatively modern, and for long incorporated the central lending library at the rear, now occupied by the Tourist Information Office. Staff had long reported supernatural happenings and an investigation was carried out in the first decade of the new millennium by a Cambridge group, WTFWT (I'll leave you to work out what that stands for!) to whom I am indebted for the catalogue of ghosts in the building. A stairway in the former library is regularly frequented by a figure identified as the ghost of a former librarian, apparently still going about his duties to the consternation of the Tourist Office staff. At the front of the building, cleaners regularly catch sight of the ghost of a man who walks to the spot where the wooden bridge used to span the road to the market hall. A town official going about his duties in the market perhaps? Another part of the building is frequented by a character who clearly had an addiction to alcohol, as the stench of vomit and alcohol occasionally assails the nostrils of persons who enter that part of the building. Most offices with a relatively large staff have someone who is known to be fond of drink, and often a blind eye is turned to alcohol related shortcomings. If this was the case with this character, then it is not difficult to see why he prefers to remain in his old place of employment where he was tolerated and can continue his drinking habits. A court once existed in the building with cells below, and these have been the site of phenomena such as the sound of something being dragged across the floor. The cell inmates cannot have been very happy in their surroundings: did the horror of their predicament make such an ingrained impression on their minds that they are still bound by their experience to that location, even after death? During and after the second world war the large hall was used for dances at which the numerous American airmen stationed in the area could mingle with the local girls. Inevitably this produced a crop of unmarried mothers—quite a social stigma at the time! The sound of music dating from that era has been heard in the hall, and communication made with an American airman looking for his pregnant girlfriend. Echoes of the past, certainly, but have the stresses of wartime produced spirits of airmen killed on active service trying to tie up loose ends from their earthly existence? Often spirits appear to be reliving some painful event from the past, or searching for something they have lost while on earth.

CONCLUSIONS OF A PARAPSYCHOLOGIST

A good proportion of hauntings seem to feature an unmarried mother looking for her baby. In past times unwanted children in poor communities were often disposed of or abandoned near a foundling hospital. One can readily imagine the anguish of a young mother forced to abandon her baby in an era when pregnancy outside marriage meant rejection by society and ruined life prospects. In the past (and perhaps still today), much was swept under the carpet and the powerful emotions generated may manifest today as a haunting. Children taken into care were often abused and died young of diseases such as TB. In this context I recall the stories surrounding the site of the old workhouse in York, now a modern housing development. The first residents were concerned by scruffy and unkempt young children seen in the evening hanging around their houses. Eventually it was realised that these were not earthly children up to no good, but the spirits of former inmates of the workhouse, whose deaths had been concealed in order to claim allowances for them from the City. Unloved in life, and with no formal burial, is it any wonder that their lonely spirits still linger around the site of their previous home?

CHAPTER 4

BELGRAVE HALL

BY TERRY HEWITT

T he Belgrave Hall saga first surfaced in December 1998. In February of 1999 I contacted Stuart Warburton, the Museum's curator, and eventually it was agreed that the ASSAP investigators should form a team to investigate the case, with myself as the lead investigator since I lived nearest to the Hall. Little did I suspect at the time that this would become a major investigation attracting the attention of the world's media! In order to ease the burden on Stuart I was asked to deal with the media aspect as I could bring many years' experience of investigations into play and had already helped with a TV programme on Coombe Abbey and its ghost. The reason for all the interest was a CCTV sequence which appeared to show the apparition of a lady in Victorian dress walking along the path which spanned the rear of the building. Once this had been shown several months later on national television news, a veritable media frenzy erupted. Stuart Warburton received telephone calls from all over the world, and at all times! I dealt with television producers on seven or more occasions. I recall a live broadcast from a studio in Nottingham, with a link to Belgrave Hall, when the mobile unit at Belgrave lost all power but the link to Nottingham still worked! I was also asked to be present when the American Doctor Larry Muntz brought a team of psychics including Derek Acorah. I tried with varying degrees of success to maintain a balanced scientific approach. A Japanese TV crew making a documentary wanted me to go rather further than I was prepared to go in an interview about the Hall's ghosts. Meanwhile Michael Lewis had been alerted by the CCTV footage on the television news, and had dismissed it as nothing more than a plastic bag floating in the wind!! Later, he was proved to be almost right, a salutary lesson for the media I feel!

Leicester City Council, the owners of Belgrave Hall, became involved. To their great credit, they decided that the Hall should be investigated scientifically, with preference being given to local groups, of which the ASSAP team would be one. It was a good opportunity to show what ASSAP could offer in terms of equipment and scientific methodology, and the team soon gained the respect and trust of the Museum. With a good working relationship established, a major investigation was planned. On a bitterly cold March evening which had seen the first snow of that winter, possibly the most illustrious gathering of parapsychologists assembled at the Hall, accompanied by the inevitable TV crew plus a reporter from the Fortean Times. The Hall buzzed with activity, and Stuart Warburton observed wryly that there were more people looking for the ghost that night than normal visitors during the day! A fox had tripped the security camera and this had frozen for approximately five seconds. Of course the workings of the CCTV security system had been examined and the problem rectified, but details must remain confidential. It was however possible to monitor the cameras from within the Hall. We were also aware that staff at the CCTV security monitoring centre were watching the proceedings, all agog, and we hoped this would not be to the detriment of other locations which were also being monitored!

The strategy was to put to the test all the possible explanations which the investigators had suggested. First off was the bat theory. This idea was my own, but it fell to a more agile Andrew Homer to climb a very tall ladder. Balanced precariously at its top, he proceeded to dangle a rubber bat at varying distances from the camera lens. By this time it had begun to snow heavily, and I was struck by how surreal the whole thing was. Those watching the cameras quickly agreed that a bat was not the explanation. It looked like . . . . a rubber bat!

Another theory which was put forward was that it could have been a moth. A moth did in fact fly by, enabling this explanation to be discounted. Next came the ASSAP Chairman, Phil Walton, with some bags of leaves carefully gathered by me from trees of different species, and particularly oak, which he let fall in front of the camera. Almost immediately it became clear that an errant oak leaf was to blame for the phantom of Belgrave Hall. As the leaves dropped slowly to the ground, there was a close resemblance to the original CCTV footage. An oak leaf was judged to give the best likeness to the CCTV footage, and indeed there were oak trees in the vicinity. Good enough was the verdict of the experts, and Stuart Warburton pronounced himself satisfied.

But this was far from the end of the ghost of Belgrave Hall. Having got our foot into the door (literally), we turned our attention to the other phenomena which are regularly reported by staff and visitors. The first task was to research the history of the Hall, and very interesting it turned out to be!

Emma Martin, then assistant curator, explains:

> *"The Hall itself only got its name around the time of the Ellis family, it wasn't called 'Belgrave Hall' it was called the 'Mansion' and various other names as there was already a 'Belgrave Hall' just off the Loughborough road, but that got burned down, around the 1840s. The name then transferred to this building. The house is approximately 300 years old, built in 1709 over a period of four years. Three very wealthy families have owned the house: the Craddocks who built it, the Vann family who were responsible for the 'Frame Work' knitting industry in this area, and enjoyed millionaire status in their day and the Ellis family who were probably the most famous family to live here.*
>
> *John Ellis was an MP for Leicester; he bought the house in 1845 and lived there with his wife and eleven children, seven girls and four boys.* **[He was a well-known farmer and respected agriculturist who turned his hand to the railways and industrialisation in general in the 1830s. Working with George and Robert Stephenson, between them they designed and ran the project for one of the first railway lines in the country, the Swannington to Leicester line which terminated at West Bridge where goods were transferred to the canal boats, for this was before the coming of the main line to Hitchin, later**

St Pancras. He became chairman of the Midland Railway Company, and died in 1862—author] *Five of his daughters bought the house from him. They were never short of a bit of money, for they were left well provided for, and they never had to work. They threw themselves into local charities, and worked with the poor houses and opened up a school for the children in the area.*

The five sisters that remained here were; Charlotte, Jane, Margaret, Isabelle and Helen. The last one to die was in 1923—Margaret, when Leicester Council acquired the property.

Charlotte was probably the most 'feisty' of them all. She really got involved with the local schools, and became a Governor of one. On one occasion she almost went to prison because of her views that the local children shouldn't have to have inoculations, because they were killing as many as they were curing. Jane was the artist! She loved the gardens and produced many designs for the eight gardeners who worked there. Generally they were the forerunners of the suffragette movement; they were part of the women's suffrage group in Leicester, and also members of the Women's Liberal Association. So they were seen as very independent and really ahead of their time."

Research conducted by the Museum staff shows that the area was mainly farmland. The house was actually built on the foundations of ten cottages which formed an L shape, and the stables at the back were part of those cottages. The house was built gradually and should not have taken four years to build, and it is believed this was because some of the original buildings were still in use or finances were inadequate.

Originally what is now the back of the house was the front, being reached by a carriage drive from the main Leicester road. The gates can still be seen, hidden away behind a profusion of flowers and shrubs.

The Talbot public house stands almost opposite the Hall and dates from the fourteenth century. The cruciform church of St Peter which dates from the thirteenth century is located next to the Hall. A former employee of the Talbot recounted how in her younger days she had witnessed the apparition of a lady in the churchyard who had waved to her and a friend, before walking through a tombstone and disappearing. Others have also reported ghostly experiences there. We always included the churchyard in our investigations with the kind permission of the vicar.

Between pub and church stands Belgrave House, another splendid historical house which at the time was also owned by Leicester Council and used for storage by the museum. It had an atmosphere of its own which was noticed when the Hall's staff had occasion to visit. A previous occupant of the House stated that she had been informed there was a tunnel between the House and the Hall, although its existence has never been verified to my knowledge. Tales of tunnels between ancient buildings are of course frequently encountered in investigations. Belgrave was very much a rural village, completely separate from Leicester. The Craddocks owned the land opposite the Hall, and also around the church and down to Abbey Lane. The Vann family, who again owned more land around the surrounding area, increased the holding which was later farmed by John Ellis.

The Vann family were prominent hosiery manufacturers in the 1870ies, and moved to Belgrave Hall from premises at Evington. They ran the business from the Hall and used the stable area as a distribution point. It was the focal point for their industry, and many of the cottages in the area had knitting machines and the locals would have been outworkers for the Vanns.

Before the arrival of the Ellis family the road outside the Hall was called the 'Cinders'. The Ellis family renamed the road 'Church Road', although as Quakers they would have had little to do with the parish church. Following the recent publicity several members of the present day Ellis family came forward, with many photographs and memorabilia of Belgrave Hall to show. The erstwhile timber firm of Ellis and Everard originated from the Ellis family, and its railway wagons and timber yards were once a common sight around the British Railways system. One such goods shed happily survives on the preserved section of the Great Central Railway at Rothley station and has recently been restored to use as a tearoom. The reopening attracted yet another member of the Ellis family who was welcomed with a guided tour. While on the subject of Rothley station, it would be remiss of me not to mention the station's own ghosts. From time to time the railway holds Edwardian evenings when the staff and visitors are encouraged to wear period dress. Some railway volunteers have said that on these occasions they have seen figures in Edwardian dress mingling with the crowds on the station platform who should not have been there, as they were not recognised as staff or visitors! Of course we cannot be sure of their supernatural origins, but it is significant that a Leicestershire battle re-enactment group also tell me that they see figures in period dress on battlefield sites whom they do not recognise and who should not be there . . . More interesting still is the story related by a volunteer who was manning the Rothley signal cabin one Friday evening awaiting the return of the dining train from Leicester North. A platelayer entered the cabin and the two men chatted for a while until the dining train approached the station. After turning away to set his signals, the signalman noticed that the platelayer had left the cabin. On leaving the cabin to collect the single line token from the engine driver (the Great Central is single track to Leicester North), the signalman realised that he had locked the cabin door, so how did the platelayer enter and leave the cabin? Had he seen the ghost of a platelayer who was killed by a train near the station? Rothley station is a wonderfully atmospheric place, carefully restored to Edwardian splendour and a delight to behold. That it should also have unseen residents is entirely fitting. The aspiring ghosthunter will want to savour its atmosphere and perhaps have tea in the restored Ellis goods shed. But I digress!

Phenomena have long been reported at Belgrave Hall. One of the most common is olfactory, often cooking smells as if the Ellis sisters are still at work in the kitchen! Emma Martin relates how soon after she joined the staff at the Hall, she was on the first floor landing when she smelt gingerbread cooking. It was a strong smell, but very localised. It disappeared when Emma took a few steps away from the landing. Curiously, co-author Michael Lewis also had an olfactory experience on this landing, but during a visit to show his wife Margaret round the Hall, rather than on a formal investigation! As the couple passed the bathroom, both were struck by the pungent smell of burning rubber. Thinking that such a distinctive smell indicated a fire risk, they told the museum assistant who was only too familiar with such accounts of strange events from visitors. Another member of the museum staff recounted how she had put some buns into the oven in the scullery (nowadays we would call it a kitchen) which is located to the side of the main building. On going upstairs she smelled a strong smell of burning while on the first floor landing, and rushed downstairs to remove her burnt buns. She was astonished to find the oven was still cold and the buns uncooked. Other cooking smells which have been reported include stewed fruit and meat.

Other common phenomena are footsteps which are heard by the staff at reception in the entrance hall below, often from the first floor. On occasions they have investigated, believing there to be no visitors in the Hall, only to find that indeed there were no visitors on the premises.

Curator Stuart Warburton was surprised when the landlady of The Talbot commented while he was enjoying his lunchtime pint that he had been working late the previous night. She explained that while walking the dog late the previous evening she had noticed the light on and the curtains closed in a second floor room used as an office. Stuart had in fact left at the normal time the previous evening, with the office light switched off and the curtains not drawn as was the usual practice. Furthermore, with the alarm system operational, any movement within the Hall would have triggered an alarm.

My co-author Michael Lewis was waiting for me to join him early one morning outside the Hall after a vigil when he heard the sound of a cupboard door being closed firmly. He then re-entered the house to check and found all the investigators putting away their equipment in the stable yard.

No-one was in the Hall and no-one had closed any doors! Dare we presume that the Hall is still watched over by unseen guardians?

The most famous apparition which has been reported on several occasions is that of a lady wearing a terracotta coloured dress. Gardener Mike Snuggs tells how he was standing in the entrance hall next to the back door when his attention was attracted by a lady in a long dress walking down the stairs to the ground floor, looking out of the first landing window, then crossing the Hall and disappearing down the passage into the scullery. The same apparition has been seen on the staircase by other members of the museum staff, who, it must be said were sceptical of the paranormal and unaware of the description given by Mike Snuggs. The initial incident prompted Stuart Warburton to keep a record of each sighting, in order to judge whether all the percipients were reporting the same apparition. Sometimes when one of the staff is dressed as Charlotte Ellis, visitors comment on a second actress in fancy dress.

The extensive, well kept gardens have an atmosphere all of their own, and it is not surprising that many psychics have sensed the presence of spirits here, Several orbs have been captured on camera in the gardens, and it is not difficult to imagine the attachment the Ellis sisters must have had to the twists and turns and secluded spots. Sitting in the gardens after dusk on a warm summer's evening is an enchanting experience. Like the Ellis sisters, the visitor of today is drawn to the mulberry tree, laden with its sickly sweet fruits.

Later developments in which I and Michael Lewis participated were "ghost hunts" when members of the public would pay to hear talks on our investigations, and were then taken on a supervised ghost hunt. Included was a supper at the nearby Talbot Inn where Michael described his sighting of a ghost in the saloon bar.

As ASSAP had become intimately involved with the ongoing investigation, it was decided to hold a Training Day at the Hall, in a property adjacent to the stables known as Cross Corners. We had not previously had access to this building in the grounds of the Hall, and obtained some good photographs of orbs in the attic. Needless to say it was hotly disputed whether dust was responsible! Further recognition of the importance of this case came when I was awarded ASSAP's Michael Bentine Shield for all the hard work I had put in (the award was inaugurated to commemorate the late comedian's role as ASSAP president).

Numerous mediums have visited Belgrave Hall, with varying and sometimes contradictory results. With all the attendant publicity, it is difficult to assess their previous knowledge of the Hall's ghosts and history. Certainly the Ellis family are well known in Leicester. But the overall picture they paint is of a happy and much loved family residence. It has been conjectured that the oft seen apparition is that of Charlotte Ellis, perhaps still loath to leave the family home of which she had many happy memories. All of the museum staff describe the atmosphere as friendly. Phenomena are ongoing. In June of 2008, museum assistant Lisa Bloor was in the entrance hall when she noticed through the window next to the garden door a boy aged about six cross the lawn. As the Hall was closed to the public that day, she wondered who it could be. Since the door was shut she looked through the window on the other side of the door, but there was no-one to be seen! More recently a colleague felt an internal door of a room she was entering being pushed against her. The latest incident concerns a musical box which was found to be playing in an empty room. It took some time and effort to wind up before it would play and of course nobody had touched it . . . .

CHAPTER 5

UFOS –
THE IMPLICATIONS
FOR MANKIND

It is possible that some people, steeped in a western culture which has no slot for UFOs, will be inclined to skip this chapter on the grounds that their interest lies mainly in ghosts and life after death. After all, aren't ufologists all eccentric characters fit only for ridicule? Hopefully you will have taken on board my comments in an earlier chapter and realise that the general attitude to UFOs is illogical and irrational. After many years of study during which I was forced into several fundamental restructurings of my tentative conclusions, I can only say that I agree with those distinguished predecessors of mine who proclaimed that UFOs represent the greatest challenge to mankind's thinking and worldview. Religion tells us that God created the world and all living creatures in seven days, Science that everything evolved from a primaeval sludge! Silvery flying discs, which have been recorded in all cultures throughout history, simply do not fit in with either theory, so they are totally ignored and anyone showing an interest in the subject ridiculed. We choose to ignore UFOs because we cannot understand them. Often the attitude is that there is no evidence of their existence, but nothing could be further from the truth.

I recall a television producer who appealed for data on UFOs for a documentary he was making. Taking the appeal at face value, ufologists provided him with boxfuls of evidence. Not one single item was used, and the programme propagated the usual viewpoint that UFOs did not exist! It is not difficult to see why this should be in our materialistic western culture. The existence of non-human intelligent beings able to build aerial craft which defy the laws of conventional science would, if generally accepted, dethrone both Science and Religion and turn our conventional world view upside down. The status quo must be maintained at whatever cost to keep the population in subjugation, for a little knowledge is a dangerous thing. The controlling elite can therefore enjoy riches, power and status. The last thing they want is for the population to realise what is really going on! So what really *is* going on?

UFOs have been with us throughout mankind's history. All cultures have recorded them, and numerous authors have documented them. It is not my purpose to set out the history and evidence for UFOs. For much of the twentieth century the conventional wisdom in Ufology was that they were spacecraft from another planet. Nowadays most researchers would accept that UFOs may be from other dimensions, and have postulated that there is a co-existent parallel universe, that is, occupying the same space but at a different rate of atomic vibration, and thus invisible to this dimension. This would explain why the occupants of flying saucers would tell contactees that they were from planets in our solar system or from other star systems. Since astronomy told us that many of these planets had features which would make them hostile to any life form as we knew them, contactees were doomed to ridicule and Ufology stagnated.

I recall that at the thirtieth anniversary celebrations, the chairman of the British UFO Research Association (BUFORA) observed that we knew little more about the mystery of UFOs than we did when BUFORA was founded! For him, that seemed to be how he wished it, although it reflected little credit on BUFORA. As time progressed, differences in viewpoint came to the fore and many members became disillusioned with the hard line sceptical stance of the association. Speakers who did not toe the party line were excluded and controversial data was discredited. It was admitted later that case files were deliberately suppressed from the membership because they were deemed too controversial! Eventually the membership voted with their feet, and faced with dwindling support as other sources of information became available through the Internet, the warring Executive were forced to wind up the association. And yet it lives! Despite the fact that I and other members passed a legally valid motion to wind up the association, elements of the former committee continue to pretend that it still exists, and peddle scepticism from what purports to be the BUFORA website. Some sceptics never give up! (Subsequent research at Companies House in London reveals that the company listed as BUFORA Ltd was wound up in 2010 by the sole remaining director).

CONCLUSIONS OF A PARAPSYCHOLOGIST

It gets worse—in 2012 BUFORA staged a 50th Anniversary Conference in London, where speaker after speaker attempted to persuade the audience that there was very little evidence for the existence of UFOs, generally trying to denigrate the whole subject. I realised to my horror that among the audience were many young newcomers who would gain an entirely negative impression of the subject and probably would not bother to pursue any further interest in the subject. In other words, the public were being deceived, *being peddled exactly the same misinformation and disinformation promoted by the Ministry of Defence!* I once declared in some exasperation that if BUFORA did not exist, MI5 would have to invent it, a reference to the known intelligence ploy of infiltrating subversive organisations to control them. With hindsight I wonder just how close to the truth I might have been in my cynicism! In recent times I have heard several stories of how witnesses have been treated by those calling themselves BUFORA. One such was entertained at a house in Ealing, where several bottles of wine were consumed during the interview; he was told that he should not pursue his UFO sighting, and when the witness subsequently suggested that BUFORA's conclusions had been affected by alcohol, he was threatened with an action for slander! An American ufologist who contacted the same people, having been told in the USA that BUFORA was the leading British UFO organisation of the highest repute, was appalled when he was given the usual brush off. Another abductee was told by a lady in Newcastle who was apparently the contact for BUFORA that UFOs didn't really exist. It was even alleged that at one time the BUFORA contact number was that of a known MI5 agent, but I cannot say what evidence there is to support this. Another (im)pertinent question might be to ask where BUFORA gets its funding from. I could certainly make an educated guess!!

One good thing to emerge from all this was that the abductee who was turned away by BUFORA ended up with a new organisation called AMMACH (Anomalous Mind Management Abductee Contactee Helpline—don't try saying this, just stick with the initials!) founded by ex-BUFORA member, Miles Johnston. They took his story very seriously and he gave a fascinating lecture at their conference. This organisation is now the cutting edge of UK Ufology and its conference is not to be missed by any serious student of Ufology who wants to know what is really going on and the true agenda of the alien occupants of UFOs. A further contrast between the two organisations is illustrated by their respective conferences: whereas the AMMACH conference was held in congenial surroundings with plenty of food on each table, BUFORA conference attendees had to endure two days in an unheated room with no food provided (obviously government spending cuts were really biting!). As always in Ufology, I have to sound a word of warning. It is the policy of AMMACH to accept the testimony of abductees and present it "as is", leaving us to make up our own minds, whereas BUFORA tried to evaluate UFO accounts by scientific investigation. This does mean that the organisation will inevitably attract delusional persons and attention seekers, but with that in mind, I have to say that some of the AMMACH abductees have provided me with the best evidence yet of alien involvement in human society.

It is now clear that the powers that be have long done everything in their power to lead people away from a belief in UFOs, and BUFORA certainly excelled in that aim. With BUFORA officially closed down, Nick Pope burst upon the scene to perpetuate the views which it had long propagated. Nick is always promoted in the press as the Ministry of Defence's UFO expert, although he never had any such title while employed by the Ministry. He resigned his job at the Ministry and became freelance. Nick carries on the role of controlling the public's appetite for UFO stories by carefully worded comments which appear to carry the stamp of authority. But it needs to be remembered that Nick was in the Ministry's front office, which fielded sighting reports from the public as a public relations exercise, and not in the back office, hidden away from prying eyes.

Nick's predecessor in the Ministry post was a woman who clearly had little interest in her post. If she was representative of the MOD's interest in UFOs, then little heed was paid to UFO reports! After Nick's departure, an answerphone system was installed for the public to leave recorded messages. Since most callers wanted an explanation from a live expert, they simply hung up. The MOD then issued a press release reporting a sharp decrease in UFO sightings which the press seized upon with delight! There are lies, damned lies and MOD statistics! With the technology available to the MOD, they must be in a far better position than anyone else to know all about UFOs, and the vacuous waffle put out by the front office can only be a smokescreen. USA beware! Nick has now relocated to the States, so US readers should watch out for disinformation cloaked by seemingly impressive credentials. Was this because no-one in the UK was buying his line?

An incident which occurred in the East Field at Alton Barnes in Wiltshire after the large crop formation had appeared on 07/07/07 reveals how dangerously exposed Nick's position is. A number of croppies (crop circle investigators) were inside the formation when a black helicopter appeared and swooped on them, firing what looked like a pink gas at them. This made them nauseous and forced them to leave. Earlier the croppies had been warned by two strange men not to enter the formation, and the farmer who owned the field had clearly also been "spoken to" as he also warned the croppies not to enter the field but refused to give any reason. This is fact, not fiction. The helicopter was photographed, and eye witness accounts tell the story graphically in a video entitled "East Field Press Conference" by Miles Johnston (a former member of BUFORA whose membership details, along with my own, were mysteriously lost in a "computer failure"). Here you have a well attested incident in which an unmarked helicopter causes actual bodily harm to innocent members of the public. A criminal offence, surely? Yet what does the MOD expert have to say about this incident? Bargepoles out! This is far too close to the mark for our Nick! No comment, he tells me in an email. Yet here we have an unknown helicopter attacking British citizens, under the noses of the MOD in an area densely covered with military bases. Almost literally over the hill is a vast army training ground where millions of taxpayers' money is spent on army war games. What is the point of all this military activity if unknown aerial craft can carry out attacks on British citizens? The fact is that the MOD simply *must* be aware of these helicopters and what they are up to. And who better to tell us than Nick Pope? If he is really interested in lending credibility to the subject of UFOs this is something for him to get his teeth into. And what does this expert say? 'No comment'. This is what all MOD spokesmen say when caught on the hop. *Is this not a strong pointer to Nick still being on the MOD's payroll? Or does he know the answer would breach the Official Secrets Act?* Consider the facts and decide for yourself. But does this disturbing incident not indicate a very worrying state of affairs? The MOD allows these helicopters to operate, it tolerates acts of war against British citizens on British soil. If it does not know about these operations, then it is scandalously negligent and asleep on the job of defending this country if attacks such as this can take place with impunity. Worse still, the affair raises the question of just who is in control of this country. You knew that John Major and Gordon Brown couldn't possibly be in control of anything, but just who would authorise attacks on their own fellow citizens?

With the realisation that UFOs were most probably ultraterrestrial rather than extraterrestrial, different avenues of research presented themselves. Gone were long, boring, uneventful skywatches. There emerged a new generation of Ufologists who had only to meditate for a UFO to appear! When I expressed an interest in a skywatch with one such, I was informed that he did not want to stay up all night and that an evening watch would suffice! I recall an organised skywatch early one evening in May at Primrose Hill, North London with Chris Martin, who has produced videos of the UFOs he has witnessed over London. On arrival one lady expressed the hope that the UFOs would soon appear as she had to leave shortly to feed her dog! Sure enough one was spotted as soon as we arrived, a white dot moving steadily through the sky under its own power at cloud level in broad daylight, a typical sighting. I felt obliged to tell a newcomer on his first sky watch that he should not regard this as the norm, as I had had to wait 35 years before seeing my first UFO!

Why bother to climb up a steep hill, when in the comfort of one's home you could channel ETs?! With the explosion of channelling in recent years, which had hitherto been confined to Spiritualist mediums contacting the dead, not only was it possible to contact Angels but the denizens of many other dimensions as well. Unlike the chairman of BUFORA, the rest of parapsychology has come a long way in 40 years. The relationship between mankind and—for want of a more descriptive word—aliens has fundamental implications for our world view. When Margaret Thatcher was confronted by Georgina Bruni, who worked for the MOD and had grasped the significance of UFOs, she responded to a plea for more openness with the words "You can't tell the people". Apparently the biggest stumbling block was that it would mean the end of the Church of England. I had some difficulty with this view, as I felt that if God had created the Universe and everything in it, then that would by definition include any creature in any other dimension. Later I realised that with all the genetic engineering which has undoubtedly gone on with *Homo sapiens*, and the different names in the Biblical account of creation which have all been translated as God (even when the plural is inferred), the traditional view of creation as propagated by the Church is too simplistic, as it is clear that the genetics of *Homo sapiens* have been manipulated many times. A simple reading of the book of Genesis, with an understanding of the terms which are all translated as God, will reveal the true origins of mankind. Few people today, less than a decade after the completion of the mapping of human DNA, remember or even accept that it showed that all members of the human race were descended from just two human beings. The Biblical account of the Garden of Eden is probably nearer to the truth than the Church likes to think. The legacy we are left with today is that half of our brain has been disengaged, so that we obediently go through the treadmill of life without the spiritual discernment which would free us from bondage. The plain truth is that we find it difficult to accept the world of the paranormal simply because our brainpower has been deliberately curtailed. The gods of the Old Testament—in reality beings from many other dimensions—have manipulated us for their own ends. Divine beings, such as Jesus Christ, have endeavoured over the ages to rescue us, so far with little success. This I believe answers the age old question of why the loving, caring God of the New Testament allows mankind to suffer so terribly. "God made man in his own image" is a very telling quotation from the Bible because it reveals that it is not God who is allowing mankind to suffer, it is mankind.

If, as Charles Fort proclaimed, we are property, then the behaviour of UFOs is readily explained. On earth, naturalists experiment with wild animals, introducing them to a new environment and then studying their reaction by electronic tags, aerial surveillance, and the occasional physical examination. Is there not an exact parallel here with the reported activities of aliens? Implants have been hotly debated, but there are thousands of reported cases. Animal mutilations, which are performed with laser-like precision, baffle us, but removal of core tissue and whole organs for analysis is exactly what we should expect if the earth and its denizens are under close scrutiny as the evidence suggests. Then there is the vexed question of phantom pregnancies. It would appear that someone is removing foetuses for research purposes or possibly genetic engineering. This is of course exactly what we are now doing, amidst a storm of controversy and strict controls. Another race would only need to be a generation or so ahead of us to have perfected this. And then there are abductions. These so alarmed BUFORA that they slapped a ban on hypnotic regression lest anyone should uncover the truth! Then they were able to proclaim that the trouble with abductions was that they were only occurring over in the United States, and not here. I fought against this ruling for years, even being told that I could not employ this technique in cases investigated for other organisations. It is true to say that BUFORA hobbled research in this country for a great many years. Did this emanate from the prejudices of a few individuals on the Committee, or was there a more sinister motive? It is now clear that mankind has been subjected to close examination for a long time, probably throughout his existence. Time after time abductees tell of being placed on an examination couch and subjected to often painful medical examinations. Samples of sperm and ova are sometimes taken which support the theory that there is an ongoing breeding programme. These are usually, but not always, carried out by the greys, some of whom seem to be little more than worker clones with few human attributes.

Many are familiar with the books of John Mack, the American psychiatrist who studied the abduction phenomenon. After his tragic death, he communicated through a medium the statement that being now in a position to find out how near to the truth he was, he wanted to say that he would not wish to retract one word from his books on UFOs!

Ufology is indeed a minefield, and all but the bravest should keep out of it. One could speculate at great length and in some detail about what might be happening, and many have done so. The man in the street will probably shudder at the wilder speculation and console himself that there is no proof. Given that our brains have had their spiritual capacity blocked off, this may be a sensible standpoint. But it does not mean that UFOs do not exist, nor that they do not have their own agenda. No wonder that the authorities are so keen to keep them under wraps. It is pointless to speculate just how much they know, because they are never going to tell us. What can be safely surmised from encounters between the military and UFOs reported many times from Puerto Rico and top secret missile bases throughout the world is that contact has occurred. It is also clear from reported sightings of strange craft around Area 51 in Nevada which perform aerial manoeuvres far beyond anything which known technology can achieve, that the USAF possesses secret aircraft which seem to display some of the technology of the UFOs. From where was it obtained? The track record of experimental aircraft using advanced terrestrial technology is dire, few if any having got beyond a prototype. Are the US military trying to back engineer a UFO from a crashed saucer, or have they persuaded the aliens to give them some secret technology?

Both scenarios are feasible in the light of known facts. Remember that it is only very recently that some of the original witnesses to the Roswell crash in 1947 have died, and documents testifying to the truth of that event (there was in fact more than one crash) have been revealed by their attorneys, since death has released the witnesses from their military oath of secrecy. I have to confess that for most of my life I did not regard the facts as proven, even though the USAF changed its explanation no less than twice. Now there can be no doubt that the USAF has possessed a crashed flying saucer since 1947, and there is good reason from the many accounts of crash retrievals to postulate that others may also be in their possession. This being so, it must be safe to assume that the US military have some knowledge of the technology after sixty years. Given that witnesses have reported contact between the occupants of landed saucers and the US military in Puerto Rico (and doubtless elsewhere as well), it is not too fanciful to suppose that they might have attempted to glean more information from the aliens about the propulsion system of UFOs. While all this may be too much to comprehend, it is nevertheless supported by solid facts. Witnesses have reported large illuminated UFOs hovering over the telescope at Arecibo. The staff manning the telescope must either have been having a night off or blind if they were unaware of this. There have been similar reports of incidents in the United Kingdom, for example the Berwyn mountain case when the military imposed a blanket clampdown on a large part of rural Wales, but the evidence is rather too patchy to be conclusive. If anyone still has any doubts in this respect, the case of the farmer whose farmhouse overlooked the field in Rendlesham Forest, Suffolk where the USAF had their famous encounter with a landed UFO in 1980 ought to banish any lingering doubts. Initially he confirmed that he had indeed witnessed the brilliantly lit object in his field, but later moved to a new farm in the West Country where he declined to say anything to investigators. Where did he get the money for a new farm, and who had sworn him to secrecy in return? Remember that my conclusions regarding UFOs are based on a critical study of the evidence for some fifty years. I have refused to speculate on what might be going on behind the scenes, only allowing myself to reach a conclusion when the facts supported them. In the case of crash retrievals I was misled by the USAF into doubting them for most of my life! Few authors on UFOs have been as conservative as this without being out and out sceptics. If you are having difficulty in taking this on board you had better avoid the many books which go much further in their assertions! And if you do not wish to be confused by facts, ought you not to be concerned that your approach to life is not governed by reason, but by prejudice! It is not my aim to provide data in support of my conclusions. There are an abundance of eminently credible books available, but I would particularly commend Ann Andrews' books "Abducted; The True story of Alien Abductions in Rural England" and "Walking Between Worlds; Belonging to None". These books chronicle the extraordinary experiences of a very ordinary family living in England and how they attracted the attentions of the British Intelligence service who burgled a neighbour's garage thinking it belonged to the Andrews! The books provide good evidence of the involvement of the British military and intelligence services who are clearly in the UFO business up to their necks. Don't take my word for it, read the books for yourself and form your own conclusions! I believe that UFOs are the key to understanding the true meaning of life and the future progress of mankind, something which is explained in a later chapter.

CHAPTER 6

CROP CIRCLES, ORBS AND MYSTERY ANIMALS

I have grouped all these topics together because I believe that all are manifestations of other dimensions. I count myself fortunate to have followed the crop circle saga right from the earliest beginnings, and am proud that I recognised the emergence of a new phenomenon right from the start, unlike many researchers who spent years puzzling over their meaning and who entered the world of the paranormal at a comparatively recent date. I recall reading the account of the Tully Saucer Nests in "Flying Saucer Review" as far back as 1966. These were circular depressions in reeds next to a lagoon in Queensland, Australia discovered after a flying disc was seen leaving the vicinity. It was readily apparent that they were made when the disc had landed among the reeds, although this one event was to cloud thinking about the cause of the later crop circles in Wiltshire.

In 1980 a report appeared in the same magazine concerning a mysterious circle impressed in a field of oats near Westbury. A researcher called Ian Mrzyglod had investigated the circle and proclaimed it of probable natural origin and of no paranormal interest. That might have been that, but a few years later the circles reappeared, in ever increasing numbers. By this time Mr Mrzyglod had left the scene, never to be heard of again, having missed his chance of fame. Given the dismissive scepticism of most researchers around that date it would be some time before the more spiritually aware researchers cottoned on to what was happening. One of the first researchers to take crop circles seriously was Paul Fuller of BUFORA. At that time I sat on the National Investigations Committee of BUFORA, and given that this august body rarely had any UFO sightings worthy of its attention, crop circles provoked an animated discussion. It was decided that as comparisons were being made with the earlier Tully case, BUFORA's job was to persuade the public THAT CROP CIRCLES WERE NOT MADE BY UFOs! To this end Colin Andrews and Pat Delgado were commissioned to mount a surveillance operation at Cheesefoot Head, near Winchester, a well known crop circle location. On the night in question, the worthy pair checked the field and then retreated to their car to escape from the rain which had settled in. The night was dark, rainy and misty, but the pair decided that if anyone was foolhardy enough to make a crop circle in such atrocious conditions their lights would surely be seen. The next day they went into the field at first light and were astounded to find a large, neat circle, made under their noses in complete darkness and without the aid of any illumination (or flying saucer, for that matter, as no aerial craft could possibly have navigated the deep bowl in the landscape with nil visibility!). Thwarted in their aim of proving crop circles were made by men with boards (clearly the fakers, obviously wearing wet suits, had nipped into the field while Andrews and Delgado were asleep, an enterprise even the SAS would have found challenging), BUFORA set out to prove that crop circles were nothing new and were in fact a meteorological phenomenon.

Paul Fuller organised a survey of cereal farmers and to his credit showed that isolated crop circles were known among the farming community long before they came to the attention of the media. In fact they went as far back as living memory, indicating that the circles had been around for a long time. Sometimes they had been found in isolated fields at harvest, having lain unnoticed for weeks. Meteorologist Terence Meaden had formulated his plasma vortex theory which postulated that in certain weather conditions columns of air could descend in valleys and leave a swirled imprint in crops. This theory at least allowed the phenomenon to grow unchecked, to the extent that when public attention was at its height, the phenomenon was able to change dramatically to large pictograms and thus gain maximum press coverage without having been stifled at birth, since the authorities had no reason to talk down what everyone assumed was a meteorological phenomenon.

I recall a conference of 200 meteorologists around this time in Europe which was addressed by Meaden. Much media coverage was given to the one meteorologist who agreed with Meaden, while it was left to "Flying Saucer Review" to point out that all 199 other delegates were firmly of the opinion that circles could not possibly be caused by plasma vortices, even if they did indeed exist! Such is public opinion manipulated. Meanwhile Paul Fuller had started a magazine called "The Cropwatcher", seemingly dedicated to the line that all circles were hoaxes. When I challenged this viewpoint, he confessed to me in private that he did believe there was a genuine phenomenon, but he preferred to investigate from behind the cover of scepticism. BUFORA was as usual doing its best to stifle the phenomenon at birth, since few of its members believed the plasma vortex theory. I recall one BUFORA meeting when Colin Andrews was billed as an additional speaker to the main speaker, a notorious sceptic. So many people turned up that BUFORA announced the meeting could not take place because of the fire regulations! A minor revolt ensued, the upshot of which was that BUFORA was grudgingly forced to move into a larger room. Full rein was given to the sceptic, and when Colin Andrews was finally rolled out, he was only allowed twenty minutes with no questions, to howls of protest from the audience. It is hardly surprising that such an organisation went out of business when the arrival of the Internet gave its members what they had always wanted but had always been denied!

The arrival of the more complex pictograms blew Meaden's theory out of the water and left the authorities caught with their trousers down. Enter Doug and Dave, two old rogues who claimed to have made all the crop circles. The media was assembled in a field in Sussex to witness the likely lads making a dreadful mess of a cornfield with ropes and planks. Experts were on hand to pontificate on the resulting formations, but could only roar with laughter at such crude circles. After this setback, the Ministry of Agriculture handed over the problem to the Ministry of

Defence, feeling that it was not an agricultural phenomenon. The MOD took a more professional approach to the problem. Since the two hoax claimants could not make a realistic circle to save their lives, a genuine circle was used to spring the trap. Experts were called to examine this circle which they duly pronounced genuine, then a press release was issued claiming that Doug and Dave had made the circle. As ever the gullible public swallowed the story whole, and interest in crop circles collapsed like a pricked balloon. I recall that attendance at meetings of the Centre for Crop Circle Studies at Kensington Central Library in London, which in the first heady days had almost filled the main hall and attracted many new faces who had not hitherto had any interest in the paranormal, dwindled to such an extent that meetings were transferred to the much smaller hall behind the stage. Doug and Dave gave a presentation in London, but such was the disdain of croppies that few attended. There was almost one fewer still, since my comment at the door that this was the first time I had knowingly paid money to a conman was met with extravagant histrionics. Around the hall were very new looking ropeboards and Wellington boots, which looked as if they had been bought that very day in Woolworths. It was very clear that the duo had no convincing answers to carefully worded questions. One croppie asked how it was that when he had been the first to walk through a virgin cornfield into a circle, Doug and Dave had somehow managed to leave no tracks; the nonplussed duo could only stammer that they had indeed walked through the corn and the croppie must have failed to notice this. Given that there were no tramlines passing through this particular formation, and the absence of a track into a newly made formation was always carefully checked by the first person entering as proof against hoaxing claims, here was conclusive proof that the pair were liars, and not very good ones either. (Tramlines is the term used to denote the bare track marks left behind by the tractor used to spray the growing crop; they are not usually found in the USA where aerial spraying is employed). When pressed they simply had no explanation for the absence of marks in the corn surrounding small circles. Another researcher quoted two large formations which had appeared on the same night in different counties, far removed from each other. How, he asked, was such a feat of bilocation achieved? Ah well, Doug exclaimed, someone else must have made the other one, blithely ignoring his earlier claims to have made them all. This charade should have convinced no self respecting researcher, yet there were present prominent members of a scientific research association who pronounced themselves satisfied with Doug and Dave's explanation. I was breathtaken at this abrogation of the protocols for unbiased investigation, but of course they were displaying the same blind belief exhibited by the critics of everything paranormal—they already had a firm, preconceived belief that all crop circles were manmade. These selfsame disbelievers later went on to "prove" that all orbs were specks of dust. Thus it is that scientific researchers cast aside all new avenues of research lest they discover anything that might contradict their own beliefs, of which more in a later chapter.

So exactly why do I believe that the MOD was so keen to divert public attention away from crop circles? The press release regarding the genuine formation which they claimed Doug and Dave had made was issued in the name of an agency which did not exist. This is a common intelligence ploy when releasing disinformation, and was used many times in Northern Ireland. A company with a similar name was tracked down in the west of England but indignantly proclaimed that they were a photographic agency and had never had anything to do with crop circles. Since Doug and Dave were unable to make a convincing crop circle, the only solution was to use a real one. The logistics of this would be formidable to anyone other than the MOD, who have access to satellite photographs of the entire country taken every hour. Since it is known that crop circles form in a few seconds, all that needed to be done was to keep an eye out for the appearance of a new crop circle and as soon as a suitable one was discovered, an expert would be rushed to the scene to be set up by Doug and Dave. Anyone who swallowed this explanation should not be reading this!

Much admirable work was done by the Centre for Crop Circle Studies. Alarmed by the hoaxing furore in Wiltshire, a team took themselves away to a quiet corner of Cambridgeshire where sporadic, simpler formations had occasionally appeared. Deducing that a local Diva (a guardian spirit of Nature, not a film star!) was responsible, the group made contact by meditation and specified a certain type of crop formation, which obligingly appeared soon after. Needless to say, the group maintained strict silence lest any local hoaxer get wind of the desired formation. Similar experiments were attempted by other researchers under conditions of secrecy, some of which produced formations which even a sceptic would agree were on target. Of course anyone who swallowed the Doug and Dave theory would no longer be in the field (pun intended!) and so would miss the repeatable experiment which for them would have been the Holy Grail. Scientific analysis quickly established certain features peculiar to crop circles which went some way to weeding out hoaxed formations, although the scientific establishment adopted their usual procedure of ignoring anything which they feared they might not be able to explain. I have always said that anyone who investigates crop circles in a totally unbiased, logical and scientific manner can only come to one conclusion. Maybe you do not want to go to this trouble, or don't have the time? Then, from the comfort of your armchair, as they say, all you have to do is to consider the formation which appeared at Barbury Castle, Wiltshire on 1 June 2008. Its design depicts the first ten digits of Pi— the ratio of a circle's circumference to its diameter. It has always been said that if denizens of another world wished to communicate with us, they would use the language of mathematics. How could any human agency manufacture such a design, and under conditions of secrecy?

At least with the phenomenon of crop circles, we have hard evidence which can be tested and analysed scientifically. Much work has been done in this field (if you will again pardon the pun) and the scientific evidence amassed is incontrovertible. Moreover, it is possible to make designs appear to order, thus fulfilling the scientific criterion of repeatability. Moreover some designs carry meaningful predictions of future astronomical events. It is my belief that events soon to unfold will show that many of the messages of the circles were warnings, warnings which only a few cognoscenti were willing to heed. I believe that the authorities (the real secret Government that is) are fully aware of the meaning and purpose of the circles, and are so desperate that they resort to gassing investigators in the circles using unmarked helicopters, ridiculing investigators, paying farmers to cut out formations, and a host of other dirty tricks. It's high time the general public looked at the facts and woke up to what is going on around them!

The question of orbs—faint, perfect circles with structured patterns within, which appear in photographs taken with digital cameras—is another example of a new phenomenon which the scientific community has been quick to scorn. Do you see a pattern emerging here?!

This time ASSAP, to its credit, did rather more than dismiss the phenomenon on the word of two geriatric hoaxers. Research was conducted with the intention of showing that orbs were dust or raindrops, and that digital photography lent itself to their production in a manner which the old cameras using film did not. Their published paper did indeed show that it was possible to produce orbs in photographs which were in fact caused by dust and particles of moisture. It therefore concluded that orbs were not a paranormal phenomenon! The research and accompanying photographs have since become a valuable source of reference for 'orbs enthusiasts' who do not want to confuse natural explanations with the real thing. However, dust and moisture may not be the only explanation for orbs as they have also been known to appear in photographs where these conditions were not present; examination with the naked eye readily reveals that orbs produced by raindrops and dust particles are rarely perfectly rounded, lack a structured interior pattern, and their size is clearly related to the distance between the camera and the object. In short they are so different from the real thing that the published photographs are used by others to emphasise how orbs cannot be due to natural explanations. Naturally it behoves even enthusiasts to carry out field tests to replicate the research's findings, and much work was done in such locations as Rendlesham Forest, a notorious spot for orbs. Members of APIS carried out tests with dust in the forest and at other locations but found it extremely difficult, if not impossible, to produce orbs by throwing sand and dust in the air. They felt that this demonstrated conclusively that dust could not be the explanation for the plethora of orbs in the forest. Not to be outdone, I conducted my own tests, which proved prolonged as dry conditions in the forest were hard to come by in the typical English summer, I found that the fine sand in the forest got into my eyes far more readily than it did into the camera lens. It was readily apparent that my camera was not capable of picking up anything as small as a speck of dust unless it was right in front of the lens. Yet when pointed into the forest, it happily recorded orbs at treetop height. And on the several damp occasions, I was careful not to take any photographs when it was raining, and always noted the weather conditions when orbs appeared to eliminate any possibility of a natural explanation. Those who did take photographs in the forest in the rain produced numerous blurred orbs which could only be interpreted as rainfall. Common sense and logic alone tell us that orbs cannot be due to rain and dust, but I am sorry to say that those who seek scientific credentials seem to be entirely lacking in these qualities. Why they do this is discussed in a later chapter.

Recently I have seen a number of orb photographs which do indeed suggest a link with some kind of spiritual entity. Some depict a cluster of orbs moving to and fro along a predefined path in haunted premises. In a haunted Hertfordshire pub, colleagues monitoring an upper room in which I was conducting a vigil with a webcam reported that they could clearly see several orbs close to my head. Seeing nothing, I moved across the room whereupon the orbs duly followed me! How can any intelligent person say they are dust particles which can only occur at a certain focal length from the camera?! Other researchers have recorded orbs moving into a séance room, or fleeing on the approach of an investigation team in haunted premises. It is possible to test out the dust theory in field conditions, where orbs are often recorded in haunted locations, and I have done this on many occasions. If the armchair theorists who promote these wonderful catch-all explanations bothered to conduct their own such tests, they would quickly realise the error of their ways. And what of the photos of spiritual gurus surrounded by a mass of orbs? Obvious hoaxes, the sceptics would say!

So what exactly is the explanation for orbs? The well known guru William Bloom has published a book entitled "Orbs Speak" in which he advances the theory that orbs are entities from another dimension who have come to assist the earth in its transition to a higher dimension. The problem with channelled communications is that they are at best anecdotal unless supported by independent corroboration, and often seem designed to fit in with concepts such as earth ascension which are not capable of verification. Other authorities opt for the explanation that they are spirits or angelic beings which at least seems feasible, if perhaps a little simplistic. What *can* be concluded is that in our present state of knowledge we are unlikely to comprehend their real nature, but what *is* quite clear is that those who attempt to write them off with such explanations as dust or raindrops can safely be dismissed.

To my eternal regret I omitted to think of mystery animals when tuned into the Knowledge Stream during my NDEs (described in a later chapter)! Once again reason and logic underpinned by scientific facts leads me to an unpalatable conclusion. What is quite clear is that the phenomenon is very real. Dead mystery animals are struck by road traffic and found at the side of the road. Such corpses have been identified as members of the big cat family. I myself have seen footage of what is clearly a North American cougar looking for its supper in a Norfolk hedgerow. The footage was so unequivocal that it was featured on the local television news. The naturalist, Trevor Beer, tiring of hearing reports of a big cat on the loose in Devon, resolved to put the matter to rest by tracking and photographing what he assumed to be a large dog. Catching his prey sitting on top of a wall one day he was astonished to have captured on film what was unmistakeably a big cat!

Statistics of big cat sightings are impressive, but the paradox is that they disprove all the current theories as to the provenance of these animals. If we take the numerous sightings of what are referred to as black panthers, for example, an impossible picture emerges. Panthers are not a separate genus of big cat, but a melanistic strain of leopard, and quite rare, existing mainly in India and parts of North Africa. Conservation is an issue because of the relatively small numbers, but even a conservative estimate of their numbers in England from sighting statistics reveals that we are apparently host to the biggest collection of panthers in the whole world!!! This simply cannot be the case. So what is going on? Unlike India, where the real thing snatches livestock and poses a problem for poor peasant farmers, the English variety rarely causes livestock depredations, and pursuits by police with rifles, helicopters and tranquillising guns, not to mention a media circus, rarely manage to catch sight of their quarry, never mind shooting it. Compare this to escapes by circus animals, which are quickly tracked down and shot. Yet the animals are all too real, nonchalantly chewing the tyres of a four wheel drive road vehicle parked in the driveway of a suburban house, to the horror and disbelief of the owner whose picture appears in the local press, grimly examining the lacerations on his expensive tyre. If his wife was the last person to use the car, how does she explain the damage to her husband (and, for that matter, to the insurance company or the garage mechanic)? There is something not quite right here, to put it mildly. When hard evidence like a corpse presents itself, the explanation that it must have escaped from its owner or been released to avoid the restrictions imposed by the Dangerous Wild Animals Act is trotted out. There is even an organisation which refuses to consider any reports of big cats before the passing of this Act in 1976 since it promotes the Act as the explanation for all sightings to the exclusion of all else, including, of course, common sense and reason, which are always the first casualties in any scientific explanation of the paranormal.

One of the unpalatable lessons I learned during my NDEs was that reality is not what it seems. As with many Fortean phenomena, I believe that mystery animals slip between the dimensions. This would account for animals which leave physical traces for a while, but then are presumed to have moved on to a fresh hunting ground or eluded pursuers armed with high tech equipment, without causing the kind of depredation among wildlife and domestic animals which is such a cause of concern in India. Similar tales are told of mystery animals in Rendlesham Forest, a known active portal area. Not all are conventional creatures, some have taken the form of a hairy monster with glowing eyes and foul breath, which is observed for a few weeks, then vanishes as mysteriously as it came. I recall a Dr Who episode in which dinosaurs were being beamed into present day England with predictable consequences. I believe something similar is happening with mystery animals, but to what purpose? As we know very little about timelines and the behaviour of atomic molecules, we are simply not able to answer this question. It has been suggested that these animals are watchers from other realms and as big cats seem to be in the majority, perhaps there is some mystical significance which we struggle to understand. Cats were, after all, revered by the ancient Egyptians and associated with the Egyptian sky gods. It is clearly a mistake to exclude mystery animals which cannot be identified with any known species, and foolish to rely on hackneyed explanations. To suggest that there are colonies of big cats native to the British Isles which naturalists have somehow failed to notice for hundreds of years is hardly feasible. When a single rare bird is spotted, birdwatchers flock in great numbers to catch a glimpse, but the same does not happen when a big cat is sighted, something which is of far greater interest I would have thought. The reason is that no-one really believes there are big cats roaming the countryside because they prove elusive after the first few sightings. The true nature of these creatures is veiled in mystery and their mere presence in the English countryside is an enigma of far greater significance than we could ever imagine.

The top still is from the original Belgrave Hall CCTV footage
(© Leicester City Council) the bottom two are enlargements
prepared for ASSAP (© Terry Hewitt). Finally identified as a wind
blown leaf, the footage provoked a media frenzy and featured on
the national TV news, but it did facilitate the ongoing investigation
of the Hall's other resident ghosts.

Bathed in sunshine, the extensive gardens add to the charm of Belgrave Hall. The ghost of a boy was seen to move across the lawn from right to left © author

From the front Belgrave Hall presents a different picture, because originally this was the back entrance, the main entrance being by means of a carriage drive from Belgrave Road through the gardens.
© author

Belgrave Hall: the first floor landing and staircase down to the entrance hall where visitors (including the author and his wife on a private visit) have smelled strange odours. © author

Leicester Museums make no secret of the ghosts of Belgrave Hall, and run regular ghost hunts. © author

Belgrave Hall: a montage in the entrance hall pays tribute to the investigations which have taken place there. © author

Belgrave *House* stands a few yards to the south of the Hall on the opposite side of the access road. It has an alluring atmosphere all of its own. Perhaps the new owners will permit an investigation, and add another chapter to the Belgrave story? © author

The Talbot Inn vies with Belgrave Hall across the road for the greatest number of spectral inhabitants. It was here that the author had his first encounter with a ghost, a truly defining moment! © author

The author poses with ASSAP President the Rev. Lionel Fanthorpe at the exact spot behind the bar at The Talbot Inn from where he watched a ghost moving around the saloon bar. © author

Terry Hewitt (right), the lead ASSAP investigator at Belgrave Hall, with fellow tutor Adam Bailey at an ASSAP Training Day held at Cross Corners, in the grounds of Belgrave Hall. © author

The fine cruciform church of St Peter, Belgrave dates from the 13th century and adjoins Belgrave Hall. Strange events have been witnessed in its churchyard, but sadly it has now been closed by the Church of England. © author

The Ellis' family business was well known in the area, as this
surviving example of one of their goods sheds at Rothley station
on the preserved Great Central Railway illustrates. © author

The splendidly restored station at Rothley has many ghost stories. Staff dressed for "Edwardian evenings" have been puzzled by ghostly extras, while a signalman in the cabin seen on the right had a conversation with a phantom platelayer . . .

Taken at a London meeting of Malcolm Robinson's Strange Phenomena Investigations organisation, the late pop star Reg Presley seems to be sharing his coffee with an orb! The author was present, but no-one noticed anything untoward. © Audrey Counsell

CHAPTER 7

HEALING

When I first qualified as an AngelTherapy Practitioner™ the angelic realm told me to work with cancer patients. I quickly located a local charity which provided complementary treatments for cancer sufferers close to my home, Barnet & District CancerLink. I was courteously welcomed and began offering Reiki treatments. Later I learned Angelic Reiki which was reckoned to be twice as effective and took half as long to administer. This therapy involves the healer "stepping back" and allowing the angelic realm to administer Reiki at a much higher vibration. Some patients were quite ill, some were undergoing chemotherapy, and quite a number had recovered but wanted to maintain a strong immune system to prevent any possibility of a recurrence. When I began to give Angelic Reiki it did seem that some patients were gaining benefit. I recall one patient who had been making a steady recovery. One afternoon I became aware that it was as if we were in an operating theatre. A number of surgeons, doctors and nurses were busying themselves round the patient. It seemed as if I was completely superfluous, but I thought I had better carry on with the customary ritual in the interests of the patient. A week or two later this patient triumphantly informed everyone that the latest hospital tests had shown that he was finally free of cancer. "I've had a spontaneous remission", he exclaimed. Actually that is a paraphrase of what he said, because I have to comply with the Cancer Act 1939 which forbids any person not medically qualified from claiming they have cured someone of cancer. In any event, I have no idea whether in reality I contributed to the patient's recovery.

Do we really have to be so unkind to cancer patients? Cancer patients have to endure invasive treatment which can make them quite ill, with no guarantee of success, so why make it difficult for them to try complementary treatments by writing it into the law of the land that only the medical profession can treat cancer? This seems to me to be a classic illustration of how the medical mafia puts the interests of medical science first, and the interests of the patients second, at the cost of untold suffering and deaths. Nearly all of my patients had undergone chemotherapy, and I spent most of my time trying to mitigate its effects rather than trying to arrest a cancer. If patients did not attend a complementary clinic, it was often because a chemotherapy session had made them too ill to make the journey. Surely there is nothing to be lost by offering patients complementary treatments, except of course doctors' egos! It would be a massive cost saving to the National Health Service if patients could be treated using other therapies, but such is the power of the medical profession and the influence of the pharmaceutical companies that patients will continue to suffer at their hands.

It does not matter to many cancer patients how a cure is effected, but it matters so much to the medical profession that they are prepared to see patients die rather than admit the potential benefits of therapies they cannot understand.

A more recent therapy which I studied is Dr Bradley Nelson's Emotion Code. The aim of this therapy is to detect and remove trapped emotions which are believed to be at the root of many illnesses by using kinesiology (muscle testing). A local Spiritualist who is qualified in most of the well known therapies told me that the Emotion Code was by far the best therapy she had come across in her long life. Intrigued I went on the course with her and was amazed at how simple and effective this therapy is. I have since treated many clients successfully, including some who had serious illnesses. In the chapter on 2012 I express the view that the second coming of Christ will be a spiritual event. One aspect of this could be the realisation that allopathic medicine does not have all the answers and that in many cases there are better, far less intrusive treatments already available. In my studies of cancer patients, I discovered that there are dozens of tried and tested remedies which could be employed at a fraction of the cost and without the debilitating effects of chemotherapy. Yet the powerful vested interests on both sides of the Atlantic never research them fully, I would imagine because they are funded by drug companies who are simply not interested in anything other than patented drugs from which they earn their profits. Many chemotherapy treatments have low success rates and do immense harm to the patient by destroying their immune systems. It is probably nearer the truth to say that most cancer patients die from the effects of the chemotherapy rather than the disease itself.

One such patient was a young sportswoman who had just passed her thirtieth birthday. When I was asked to do an Emotion Code session with her I discovered a string of past traumatic events which had undoubtedly caused the cancer. Unfortunately she had undergone extensive conventional treatment, and secondaries had set in which dictated the final outcome. The irony is that had she been treated with the Emotion Code and not endured the terrible suffering inflicted by conventional medical treatment, her life would probably have been saved. Yet the current view of society is that I am a dangerous nut who tries to dissuade cancer patients from life saving treatment! Nothing could be further from the truth, but a sea change in attitudes and opinion could result in a vast saving to the UK's National Health Service (which would be most welcome in the current straitened financial times), and significantly improve survival rates in cancer cases without causing harm and distress to the patient.

I recently attempted to promote the Emotion Code at a so-called Complementary Therapies centre for cancer patients, which was supported by a national cancer charity, and had just opened at a major London hospital. I was fobbed off (sorry, referred) to the two National Health managers responsible for setting it up. Neither bothered to even reply to me! Was this just incompetence, or was it because both charity and centre were funded by the drugs industry? It is a truly shocking state of affairs that the medical profession and national cancer charities are only interested in promoting an expensive, frequently ineffective and harmful form of treatment, and see complementary therapies only as palliative treatments for patients they have harmed. They have even banned the promotion of alternative cancer treatments under the Cancer Act, 1939, for the purposes of boosting scientific egos and the profits of drug companies. When oh when are people going to awaken to what is going on, and how they are being cheated and mistreated? If this is one effect of the new energies then they will truly be to the great benefit of mankind.

I would sincerely urge anyone who is given a diagnosis of cancer to consider alternatives to conventional medical treatment. I firmly believe that a patient who opted for one of the cancer diets coupled with something like the Emotion Code would stand a better chance of survival. Nor should such treatment be considered as an adjunct to conventional treatment, which in my view does more harm than good in many cases. The least you can do is to read one of the many excellent books available on alternative cancer treatment, such as "Cancer Free" by Bill Henderson, and make up your own mind. The UK's Cancer Act requires me to make it clear that I am not offering a cancer cure—would that such a cure did exist! If any UK cancer sufferers are interested in other forms of treatment, I can be contacted through my website, but I must emphasise that in cases where conventional treatment has been given it is unlikely that alternative treatments may offer any relief.

What is not generally understood by the public is the contribution which complementary therapies can offer to the alleviation of suffering, often in cases where they have only been employed as a last resort because conventional medicine seems powerless. When such therapies do prove efficacious, it is often because they address what I will term the spiritual cause of an illness. Is it any coincidence that people who suffer a severe emotional trauma, such as the loss of a loved one, sometimes develop cancer? One of the problems with medical science is that they concentrate on treating the symptoms of an illness rather than the cause itself. True, some illnesses are caused by bacteria which can be eliminated by the use of antibiotics, but even the explanation of bacteria as a cause of illness is not as simple as it might seem. It is a well known fact that in an epidemic far more people will be carrying the bacterium concerned than will actually develop the illness it can cause. This clearly demonstrates that thought patterns and negative emotions can contribute to illness. Illnesses may have a wide range of origins, so cancer may have many different causes. This is where complementary therapies can be of assistance. By reading the body's subtle electromagnetic field, known as the aura, the therapist can often get a good idea of the origin of an illness, and then treat the out of balance chakra which regulates the area concerned. The cause of the imbalance in the chakra can then be investigated by reference to factors which are known to affect that particular chakra. These might be karmic, i.e. past life issues, or collective or ancestral issues. This is largely unexplored territory and it is unwise to assume that a health problem is karmic. More likely causes are lifestyle issues, including diet, but an issue of increasing importance is mindset. A person who takes a pessimistic, negative attitude to life is far more likely to suffer increasing health problems. On the other hand, a person who adopts a healthy, happy lifestyle but still falls ill is likely to have suffered an emotional trauma in their life which remains unresolved. This demonstrates the falseness of the argument that an unhealthy lifestyle is justifiable because those with a healthy lifestyle also suffer from ill health!

I would suggest that anyone contemplating seeking complementary treatment should seek out therapists who work by reading the body's subtle energy fields, and also those channelling higher entities (not just deceased relatives) who can often detect a spiritual cause for an illness. Once you have obtained a firm diagnosis as to the cause, it is much easier to locate a therapist who specialises in a particular area. A few words of warning are necessary here. Well known figures in the New Age movement who charge large sums are best avoided, if only because the patient cannot really afford them. As a general rule, once someone hits the big time with the riches it brings, spiritual considerations are outweighed by monetary considerations, and decline sets in, although the therapist may continue to practice on the strength of a past reputation which is no longer justified. There are many gifted therapists hidden away in Spiritualist churches and circles who shun the limelight, if only because of the derision they would attract from sceptics. An unassuming therapist with little thought of personal gain can often achieve better results than a famous guru. With channels it is a question of finding someone who appeals intuitively to you. You will often be attracted to channels who are in communication with the particular realms in which you have previously been incarnated. Beware ego-driven channels! If you cannot accept what a channel says or dislike his style, then look elsewhere. Always do your homework before you choose, research your therapist or guru on the internet, find out what others say and perhaps attend a lecture or workshop with them before making up your mind. When assessing the opinions of others it is vital to understand their own personal stance, since a notorious sceptic is unlikely to say anything good about any complementary therapist. Some parapsychologists have a bee in their bonnet and will offer the same opinion on almost anything regardless! Others will automatically reject anyone who charges a fee, but of course this ignores practical issues such as the rent of therapy rooms.

CHAPTER 8

NEAR DEATH EXPERIENCES: A PERSONAL EXPERIENCE, AND THEIR IMPLICATIONS

O n a sunny summer's day in August 2006 I set out to Wiltshire for a conference on Crop Circles in the delightful surroundings of Marlborough College. Little did I know what was in store, yet the preceding weeks had been ominous. As an AngelTherapist™ I work closely with the angelic realm, and that summer had seen nothing but disappointments. It seemed I could make no progress in my work. To cap it all, the angels seemed to be like birds roosting at sunset, fading into the background. Whenever I tried to console myself that at least I was in good health, there was nothing but silence from the angelic realm. The day before my departure, they had told me to cut the lawn, even though I had decided it didn't really need cutting. I was overwhelmed with foreboding. Something momentous was brewing, I had never had such a strong feeling before.

As I prepared to leave, the angels told me "You might not be coming back, you might die suddenly while you are away". Taking this as no more than a reminder of human mortality, I shrugged it off.

No sooner had I reached my destination, I went down with the prevalent summer gastric virus (the notorious *norovirus*). Feeling better the next day, I went to the Conference, but as the day wore on it became apparent that I was going downhill. I did all the right things, seeing a doctor at the local cottage hospital, and retiring to my hotel. Two days later, on leaving my hotel for a breath of fresh air, I felt extremely unwell and collapsed in the street. The community ambulance had intended returning me to the cottage hospital, but soon discovered that my bodily systems were shutting down and took me to the district hospital at Swindon instead. I did not respond to treatment too well, and contracted pneumonia, becoming extremely ill. At this point my heart started to fail and there began a most extraordinary succession of Near Death Experiences (NDEs).

I had been moved to the Heart ward, although I did not know why, as I had been monitored under the heart disease prevention programme with my GP and at Barnet Hospital, and been given a clean bill of health. Lying in my hospital bed, propped up and connected to various pieces of medical equipment, I resigned myself to a restless night. After a while I did manage to fall asleep, but immediately became aware that I was somewhere else. First, it had a dreamlike quality. I was in the company of a man who was showing me around what can best be described as a Hall of Learning. It was like a vast reference library, and I was able to choose whatever topics I liked. The guide then explained the topic, which was usually connected with religion or the paranormal. The guide then bade me farewell, telling me that I could return any time I wished. I then woke up again, but feeling more relaxed, and soon returned to sleep.

At once I found myself fully aware, completely out of my body. It was like nothing I had ever experienced before and I knew that I had passed into Spirit. The first thing I did was to march up to the Reception Desk.

Before I continue, I would like to pause here because I must at this point try to explain that in the spirit world one communicates using only the mind, and the images you can see in this world are subjective. It is difficult to understand that in spirit form our consciousness continues to exist, when we are so accustomed to a physical world and have been indoctrinated with the belief that consciousness is a product of the brain. In fact the computer which was remotely monitoring my heart recorded that my heart had failed, and in these circumstances medical science states that there can be no brain activity and therefore no consciousness of anything. I am afraid that medical science is plain wrong!

To resume the narrative, I was a little irritated not to be greeted by St Peter, but nevertheless asked "Do I get to see God?" I don't know why I asked that question, as I had not prepared for my death, although I was fully aware of what had happened to me and where I was. The answer surprised me: "You are God". I immediately realised the significance of the doctrine of the Brotherhood of Man. Realising that I was now in a position to find answers to the questions which had long eluded me in my study of parapsychology, I asked my guide how the various religions of the world fitted in with the scheme of things. He produced a long list and then proceeded to dismiss them all, one by one, as manmade. When he got to Christianity, he asked me what views I held about my own religion. I realised that the basic tenets of belief resulted from the Council of Nicaea, when votes were taken and certain beliefs were outvoted. I thought of the Synod of the Church of England, when Archdeacon Garth Moore assembled those opposed to the ordination of women and ordered them to glare at the supporters of the motion. He succeeded the first time, but the motion was reintroduced subsequently and passed. Doubtless similar tactics were used at the Council of Nicaea, as it is known that the supporters of differing beliefs ganged up on their opponents. I did not feel able to argue that gatherings such as these could possibly be defended as the will of God, and conceded the point.

I was then plugged into the Knowledge Stream from which knowledge of every conceivable topic could be readily obtained. This is a difficult concept for us to understand. It can best be likened to the telephone points which are installed in banks, from which information on any of the bank's services can be obtained by ringing different numbers. Alternatively it can be viewed as akin to a download from a huge computer database. I asked many questions about paranormal topics, from UFOs to crop circles. My guides congratulated me on how knowledgeable I was, and how I had followed the right path in my researches. Very few people bothered to gain such insight, they said. But in reality they were just being kind to me, as I soon realised that I had not really travelled very far along the path of knowledge during my earthly incarnation. It grieved me how much I had rejected due to my scientific scepticism, and lack of a broader vision with lateral thinking. Those whose outlandish beliefs I had rejected out of hand were closer to the truth than I had been. Nevertheless it was apparent that those who study the paranormal have a head start on the rest of the pack, and get off to a flying start because they know what has happened to them at death. Of course many adherents of scientific research organisations could never accept their continued existence after death, and must have great difficulty in coming to terms with such a complete reversal of their beliefs. I am haunted by a sad vision of the chairman of one such organisation, walking away from me in the opposite direction, with his back to me as he walked away from the light. Precisely what I learned is too vast to enumerate, but I was gratified to be told that my conclusions regarding the origins and purposes of crop circles were correct and did not need any further elucidation! My request for confirmation that God did make the Universe was met with some amusement as I had already worked that out for myself, but finally I was told "He did". I did manage to ask about earth changes, and these were confirmed although no details were forthcoming.

At this point I must interject that during my stay in hospital I drifted between the worlds and the chronology of a succession of NDEs is indeterminate, I would imagine because time does not exist in the next dimension. Further, the relationship between the experiences is not always easy to determine and some experiences appeared to contradict other experiences. Thus it is, and I can only assume that it must be very difficult to grasp the depth and scope of what awaits us on the other side. There were differing aspects of the NDEs, and some seemed concurrent. During the time when the hospital computer recorded that my heart had failed I found myself on a conveyor belt in what resembled a hospital Accident and Emergency department. I was told that I had been recalled to HQ for a briefing, but I had a problem which would have to be attended to. I presumed this referred to the heart problem, but on this occasion I did not demur as I had done when hospital doctors made this diagnosis! I was told that all new arrivals were examined to see if anything could be done for them, but that hopeless cases were allowed to pass on. I had come from a hospital, as did many others. I have absolutely no recollection of any surgical procedures, and then underwent a lengthy experience, the nature of which I was sworn to secrecy. At the end I enquired what would happen if I did break my promise of secrecy, as I was acutely aware of the effect which a lecture on the subject to fellow parapsychologists would have! Scornfully, I was asked if I thought anyone would believe me, a point which was all too apparent. During this experience, various clues were given to me which "they" knew I would follow up. Although unravelling them occupied the next two years, I then realised just how significant the answers were in terms of world religions, the origins and history of the human race. The realisation of how things were and the implications for civilisation as we know it were mind shattering. I was then returned to the body by a means which was arguably the most significant experience of my whole life. Re-entering my body was like getting dressed in a set of cold, soaking wet clothes and was so unpleasant that I half wondered whether I was sensible to return. I was told the next morning that according to the computer monitor my heart had failed several times during the night, although no explanation was proffered as to why no action appeared to have been taken by the medical staff.

I remained in hospital for eleven calendar days, although I actually spent 12 days there! A few days after my first NDE, I went through a second, rather different NDE. After falling asleep, I again found myself in another dimension. This time I was shown the Hall of Records, otherwise known as the Akashic Record. Somehow the teachings of Christ on this subject had failed to sink in, and I was rather surprised to discover that this did indeed exist. It was shown to me as a massive card index system. I was somewhat amused by such outdated technology, although it must be realised that in a mental world everything is figurative. My guide extracted the top card of my record, on which was depicted a photograph of myself and the inscription "Michael Lewis 1946-2006". I cannot now recall whether the photograph showed me without the glasses which I had had to wear for most of my life to correct myopia, or whether it showed me with only the reading glasses round my neck, a very recent development following several operations at Moorfields Eye Hospital. I was invited to review the contents of the card file, but declined to do so as I reckoned I was already well aware of the course of my life! I have often wondered whether this was the correct decision, as this might have been intended to make me aware of my shortcomings which I could then address.

At this point it came home to me that I had really passed over (presumably from heart failure and pneumonia). I was well aware of my surroundings and what I was now experiencing. I was able to communicate with the angelic realm with crystal clarity, all was purity and truth. I realised just how cloudy and imperfect communication between the earthly and higher realms really was by comparison. I had no inclination or desire to return to such a dense and imperfect bodily existence. Now I have to say that I was in a blissful state, luxuriating in a higher energy vibration where I had access to knowledge on anything I wanted—and there weren't half a few surprises! I remarked to the angels how much better my existence had become, although I realised how much of a shock my unexpected death at an early age would be to those left behind, especially to my wife and children who clearly had not appreciated the seriousness of my condition. I doubted that my wife would be able to cope (this was subsequently proved to have been correct, as she ran out of money after a few days despite the safety net I had put in place for just such an eventuality), and felt that just as I was entering the most fulfilling phase of my life, I had been robbed of life with my mission only just started. I recall bemoaning that I had worked for 38 years and only lived to draw three months' pension! Regretfully I decided that I must return, and asked the angels if this was possible. They replied that there was something they could try, a response which I did not find entirely encouraging! I then asked them how this was physically possible, since I reckoned I had been dead for about a day and irreversible chemical changes would have occurred at cellular level. If time was turned back a day so that I could have a different outcome, then I assumed that everyone in the world would have to relive the same day just for me, and we would forever be doomed to endure the same day over and over again as there would always be someone who did not want to die that day. It was explained that this would not be necessary, as only a very few people involved in my care would have to have their perceptions of reality altered. The angels showed me a conveyor belt, with markers representing days in our time. "You are aware that time does not exist in reality", they told me. I did, but how this could be had always eluded me. To demonstrate the point, they picked an object off the conveyor belt and replaced it further back along the belt. "You will have to relive the day you died again", they warned me, which I felt I could cope with. Sure enough, on waking in the morning it soon dawned on me that I had indeed lived that day before! My wife brought me "The Telegraph" but on turning the pages I realised that I had read them already! Feeling unable to say that I had read it yesterday, I had to pretend to read the paper all over again, before passing it to my fellow patients. That night I waited in fascination for the patient in the farthest bed to return the paper to me. Sure enough, he did so and I had to resist the temptation to say that I did not want it back a second time!!! That day (the second time round, that is) I felt sleepy after lunch, but mindful of what had happened when I fell asleep the first time round, I felt it was wiser not to fall asleep. However, the angels told me that I would be fine now and it was a good idea to get some sleep.

The next day the heart consultant told me that he would undertake an angioplasty on my heart, as it was advisable to strengthen the heart muscle. He explained that both the major heart valves were failing and I got the impression I would soon die if this action was not taken. Since I was aware that the heart problem had been dealt with by beings from another dimension, I did not want any interference from earthly doctors. I felt it wiser not to explain matters lest I be transferred to the psychiatric ward, so consulted my guides as to how on earth I could get out of this situation safely. We decided that I would have to leave the body, as the consultant would not operate if he thought I was dead!

And so it was that when the medical team approached my bed the next morning I made no response. Accompanied by my guide, I descended, metaphorically speaking, to the basement, clutching a treasured family heirloom which I think was symbolic of the attachment we have towards earthly treasures. The guide opened the trap door in the floor, we left, closing the trap door behind us. This was, I think, symbolic imagery relating to the base chakra. I could then hear everything which was being said by the medical team. After failing to rouse me, a specialist team was summoned and proceeded to go through the procedure for declaring a patient dead. All other patients were removed from the ward. Boiling liquid was poured into my ears, and I heard the team leader remark that it was a severe test and I had showed no response. Pepper was then sprinkled on my right wrist. The plan was that when they got to the stage of declaring me dead, I would groan theatrically and open my eyes, which it is what I did. Obviously certain drugs had been injected in me as another team spent the next hour carrying out various procedures to counteract their effect. Finally the heart consultant was allowed to see his patient, and lamented to his assistant that the angioplasty could not now be undertaken. Plugging me into a computerised heart scanner he examined my heart. He then exclaimed to his assistant "I do not see today what I saw yesterday!", and then pronounced that both heart valves were functioning correctly. I could of course have enlightened him, but stuck to my policy of saying nothing! I had persuaded my wife to take a break sightseeing in nearby Marlborough that morning, so she was unaware of the morning's events. That afternoon several relatives visited me, although I felt far from seeing anybody. Thereafter a slow recovery ensued, during which a new doctor read up my case notes, examined me, and then said she could not understand what I was doing in hospital! I merely reiterated the circumstances of my illness.

A month after my discharge from hospital I was recalled for a review. I took the opportunity to enquire whether my heart was now functioning correctly after such a serious double malfunction, and how this had been achieved, knowing full well what had actually happened! The doctor was bemused and went off to see the heart consultant. He was equally puzzled, so they spent some time reviewing the test results which confirmed that I had indeed been very seriously ill. They assured me that all was now well with my heart, and could only suggest that the condition had been brought on by pneumonia and "had righted itself" when the pneumonia subsided. Not so, as a Chinese medicine practitioner had diagnosed a heart problem before I had become ill, and if heart conditions healed themselves, heart consultants would be out of a job! Again I maintained silence.

On reflection it occurred to me that I had never interested myself in "Timelines" which I had dismissed as a fanciful New Age concept. Several colleagues drew my attention to the film "Groundhog Day" in which the hero keeps reliving the same day. I had never heard of this prior to my NDEs. Anecdotally, I was informed by one guru that not everyone is on a variable timeline, which might explain why the angels were unsure whether it would be possible for me to return. I was also told that subsequently all timelines became fixed as we approached 2012, and changes such as I had been allowed were no longer possible.

The implications of what I had learnt took a long time to sink in. Perhaps the most profound and worrying was the realisation that *reality as we perceive it does not exist!* Quite apart from anything else, that alone would cause any red blooded scientist to either shoot himself or (more likely) burn the offending book in a consuming rage. I recall laughing at the suggestion by one guru that the Universe does not exist, we make it all up as we go along! *To my horror, this explanation of the Universe fits in best with my own NDEs, although it does offer some respite from the problem of how the Universe can be infinite.* The idea of timelines and how they interrelate is totally beyond my comprehension. What happened to the nurses who would have laid out my body in the hospital mortuary? Did they too have to relive the day? And was this extra day confined only to those directly involved with my death? All that can be said is that our restricted brainpower is insufficient to process this information, although a quantum physicist might be able to make a few tentative suggestions.

CHAPTER 9

THE PROBLEM WITH SCIENTIFIC RESEARCH SOCIETIES

I t will have become clear that the shortcomings of conventional science have been a recurrent theme of mine. I need to make it clear that it is not Science itself with which I have a problem, but the entrenched attitudes of scientists. Science comes from a Latin word meaning Knowledge. Most researchers say that they are on a quest to understand the paranormal, or, as they term it "The Truth". In theory there should be no difference between truthseekers and scientists since both ought to have the same goal: first establish that an effect can pass the test of repeatability, then study it to find the cause. This is what parapsychologists have always done. I started my career in parapsychology with the usual western attitude that UFOs did not exist and that people who claimed to have encountered them were mad. But by taking what I considered to be a scientific approach, that is, by studying the quality and volume of the evidence, and the mental state of witnesses, I soon came to the conclusion that there was indeed a phenomenon worthy of scientific study. Many years of research, hampered by rigid western belief systems and attitudes, led me to begin to understand that UFOs represented something of immense significance for mankind. I have to say, however, that never in my wildest dreams did I guess at what was revealed to me in my NDEs. The truth is so far removed from current scientific beliefs, the gulf so deep and unbridgeable, that there is no chance whatsoever of scientists ever accepting such a seismic shift in their beliefs. I was in fact told not to bother trying to reveal the truth, rather to live the remaining few years quietly at home!

I have come to realise that scientists do not study everything according to strict protocols, they pick and choose in order to boost their own egos, and disregard anything which they are not clever enough to explain, regardless of the fact that this is only because they do not have the necessary measuring instruments. It gets worse. The early scientific pioneers made many errors, but are lauded and like the Pope regarded as infallible. Newtonian physics is considered to be the Holy Grail within mainstream scientific circles, but in reality it has provided a springboard from which a rather different kind of science (based on Quantum physics) has evolved which largely invalidates much of what Newton taught. This is readily apparent to today's scientists, but woe betide anyone who dares to question the Master!

Archaeology is a poisoned chalice, since its origins were tainted by religious beliefs about the creation of the world and the history of its peoples. It is a fact that modern dating techniques have shown the pyramids of Egypt to be much older than archaeologists believe because in the early days they were constrained by then current religious tenets about the age of the earth, notably Bishop Ussher of Armagh who carefully worked out from the chronology of the Bible that God created the world in 4004BC!! Therefore nothing could have existed prior to that date! It is quite incredible that scientists can still cling to disproven ideas simply because of the convention that the hallowed tenets of the past must not be questioned! The fact is that modern Science has taken over as the new religion from the Church of yesteryear. Like the Church, it has hallowed tenets from the past which no-one must question, even when shown to be plain wrong. Its adherents must toe the line at all costs, otherwise rejection and loss of livelihood will follow.

The root of the problem lies in the Ego of scientists. I use the capital E deservedly. If the existence of other realms inhabited by beings who can display a far superior technology (I am referring to UFOs and aliens of course) were to be admitted, then immediately the scientific Gods of today are dethroned and shown to be no more than primitive beings with rudimentary ideas about the Universe, a far cry from the status they currently enjoy of being the most intelligent creatures in the whole Universe! A classic example of the point I am trying to make is the case of the Bosnian pyramids. Recently three pyramids were "discovered" near the town of Visoko in Bosnia (they had been regarded as natural features because of their overgrown state). Excavations and much scientific research have been undertaken which show that the sides are lined with cut stones, and underground tunnels and chambers have been discovered. Of course the pyramids have always been there, covered with a thick layer of soil and greenery. But there can be no doubt whatever that what we have here is a pyramid. Yet the scientific community has turned its back on the pyramids, the Bosnian government has obstructed excavations, and some scientists claim that the structures are *natural formations!* The arrogance and stupidity of the scientific fraternity in this respect is breathtaking, and if the public were given the facts, there could be no doubt about the authenticity of the pyramids. The problem is that, having been hopelessly wrong about the dating and origins of the Egyptian pyramids, the Bosnian pyramids cannot be made to fit scientific paradigms. So therefore they cannot exist! Simple! The scientific ego would be mortally wounded by being proved wrong. Research triggered by the discovery of the Bosnian pyramids has revealed pyramids in Spain (explanation: farmers clearing their fields of stones for cultivation piled them up in a pyramid shape), and underwater stepped pyramids in the sea off Japan (explanation: rock formations worn into precise geometric shapes by the sea). Once an erroneous scientific belief has been established, the Scientific Ego will go to any lengths to defend it.

The tragedy of all this is that the public are spoon fed the idea that scientists can explain everything and that anything which appears to be outside the realms of science can safely be dismissed as nonsensical.

The media rarely refer to anomalous phenomena and only then in a lighthearted, flippant manner. The BBC is bound by its Constitution not to refer to anything anomalous in a serious manner, but is duty bound to denigrate and ridicule it. How gleefully have I pointed this out to pretty young things from the BBC with an idea for a serious programme on some aspect of the paranormal, who are naïve enough to believe that the BBC has freedom to report anything it likes! As in the days when the Church held its sway over large parts of the earth and the population dutifully believed what they were told to believe, nowadays Science deceives the population for its own ends. How inconvenient it would be if the population woke up and started to ask serious questions! The fact is that *Homo sapiens* was genetically engineered with a brain which has been programmed to carry out the whims of its masters in humble subservience, but with little comprehension of the spiritual side of things. It is outside the scope of my remit which is based on scientific enquiry and methodology, to speculate on the religious beliefs current today, but if mankind really is about to awaken from a long slumber and cast aside erroneous belief systems, then I for one will give three cheers!

Scientific research societies find themselves in a cleft stick. They feel that psychical research should be conducted and presented according to scientific protocols. Fine—the problem is that the subject is frowned upon by the scientific community, so the only way parapsychologists can gain the scientific respectability they crave is to produce entirely negative findings. Thus it was that crop circles and orbs were promptly dismissed by ASSAP to gain credence in the scientific world, and two very important developments were sidelined, preventing any findings which might not meet with approval by the scientific world. (ASSAP will of course point out that it does not hold any corporate views but this is a convenient escape clause). In 2010 ASSAP hosted a large conference at very reasonable cost to announce that it had been appointed by the Government as regulator for ghost hunters. At least they actually admitted it! It was never explained how this had come about and what the implications were, although needless to say the conspiracy theorists had a field day! As far as I was concerned it meant that it was now less likely that ASSAP would do or say anything which might embarrass the government or upset the status quo, in other words it had been corralled. I once attended an ASSAP training course when we were told that most paranormal occurrences had a natural explanation and that the remainder could not be proved scientifically so should not be claimed as paranormal, thus slamming the door on any meaningful progress. This probably explains the high turnover of membership in these societies, as members quickly become disillusioned and turn to pastures new. The problem is that they often end up in organisations which are led by gurus who indoctrinate their followers, or enthusiastic amateurs who adopt an entirely uncritical approach. This means that the benefits of a scientific approach are lost, and any positive results dismissed accordingly. Like Science, the field is often ego driven. I have lost count of how many groups I have known which have split up because of conflicting egos, usually fading away because the splinter groups lack viability. I have also known many flourishing groups which have become moribund because the leading light moved away or became distracted by family concerns. The point is that a national group like ASSAP is not likely to be affected in the same way, and can provide continuity and promote higher standards. But ultimately such groups must choose either to languish on the fringes of science or renounce their basic aims! Groups which choose the former will never make any significant progress, if only because science does not have instruments which can measure and record other dimensions invisible to this dimension, because they vibrate at a different atomic frequency (although the Hadron Collider project does begin to address this problem). Groups which choose the latter will make progress, but it will go unreported and unrecognised. The late BUFORA took the former course and recorded very little progress in the forty or so years of its existence. Its members were led carefully along a path which shielded them from anything which might have provided an answer to the mystery of UFOs. It is only since its demise that the real picture has emerged through such ventures as the UFO Academy initiated by the charming and spiritual O'Neill sisters at their home, High Elms Manor, Garston, near Watford (formerly known as Garston Manor), although I must admit to having had the opportunity through my NDEs to get the full picture.

The Centre for Crop Circle Studies did, to its credit, carry out research which got to the bottom of the phenomenon, but then did not really know how to handle findings which did not conform to the science whose principles it had used in its researches! These findings pointed firmly to a world of beings from other dimensions making intelligent communication with us and warning us of future events of which we needed to be aware. This was too much for some researchers to cope with, and preferring to bury their heads in the sand they withdrew from active involvement, not wishing to be seen to rock the scientific boat. This brings us to a crucial point: if mankind's consciousness is raised to bring an appreciation of unseen worlds, the cultural shock is likely to be so profound to those who have been controlled by science and religion that many will feel unable to continue with any meaningful life, being in a position similar to those who waste away from unrequited love. Since such a radical shift in consciousness is outside the experience of the current world era, it is impossible to predict the consequences for society other than that they can only be profound.

CHAPTER 10

ENCOUNTERS WITH SPIRITUALISM

I t would be true to say that it was Spiritualism that first aroused my interest in the paranormal, but it would also be true that I have always been fascinated by the idea of ghosts. It was a natural progression for me to attend Bedford Spiritualist Church as soon as I reached the age of 16. Often I was given an unfamiliar name, but on enquiring around the family I was usually able to identify accurate details about the communicator. This taught me two important lessons: one, that sitters often failed to recognise communicators because of lack of knowledge of their family history; and two, drop in communicators who have only a tenuous connection with the sitter often present themselves, simply because they are desperate to make their presence known, sometimes asking for messages to be passed on to others. This leads me to believe that scientific investigations of mediums are incomplete because reliance is usually placed solely on whether the sitter can recognise the communicator. This means that statistics for "hits" (correct information) are likely to be universally understated, to the extent that the general public gains the impression that mediumistic communications are usually vague and meaningless. This of course suits Spiritualism's many detractors admirably, since they are only interested in negative data, and having found what to them are grounds for their disbelief, have no inclination to delve any deeper. Once again an unbiased, objective assessment is lacking.

Deciding to find out the views of the Orthodox Church on the question of an afterlife, I joined the Churches' Fellowship for Psychical and Spiritual Studies, as it later became. It was able to offer me an unofficial version of the Church of England's report into Spiritualism produced in 1939, published by the Spiritualists. As it was favourable to Spiritualism, it was of course suppressed by the Established Church, ostensibly due to the outbreak of war. Eventually the Church was shamed into publishing it many years later, long after the Spiritualists had placed it in the public domain. It soon became apparent that there were within the Fellowship the usual bitter divisions between the Religious Establishment and those who took a more enlightened view. Eventually the Establishment succeeded in gaining the upper hand, adding the word 'Spiritual' to the title in order to dilute the intentions of its founder, Colonel Reginald Lester. Committees which might actually have produced reports favourable to psychic phenomena were ruthlessly suppressed, to the extent that committee papers were snatched from the noses of committee members by the General Secretary, Maurice Frost, whose pernicious role in the suppression of truth earned him the nickname of "The Blighting Frost"! The Headquarters Fund was amalgamated into other funds in a bid to stop a London HQ which would be a thorn in the side of the Church. This was successful, as the Fellowship is now established in a bleak, windswept Nature Reserve in a desolate part of Lincolnshire, out of harm's way, and firmly under the thumb of senior church dignitaries!

Connections with mainstream Spiritualism were intermittent after I moved to London, perhaps because I needed no confirmation of the veracity of Spiritualism, preferring to work within the mainstream churches. Until I qualified as an AngelTherapist™, that is! It was the Christian church which had taught me about the concept of angels, but when I told of my work with the angelic realm I was told quite firmly that I was nuts. There was little point in staying within a church which discouraged its adherents from the doctrines it preached, and I was left wondering just what, if anything, the church actually stood for. Is it perhaps a Sunday morning social club to make you feel good, as an alternative to the gym or the golf course perhaps? And so I became a card carrying member of Barnet Christian Spiritualist Church. It soon became apparent that the only way to identify the plethora of names recited by mediums was to get a copy of my family tree. This resulted in a dramatic increase in the recognition of spirit communicators. Another problem with communications was a tendency of spirits to refer to long forgotten incidents. One such communicator was my paternal grandfather, communicating with me on one of many occasions, who reminded me of an incident in which my grandmother had caused a fire in the kitchen of their home, which had resulted in the attendance of the fire brigade. I struggled valiantly to recall this incident, about a century ago now, and only succeeded because the kitchen fire was so well known in the family during my childhood that I was able to recall my parents laughing about it. Mediums are often criticised for relaying communications which the sitter cannot understand, but how many people know of or can remember distant members of their family or incidents which took place long ago?

I feel that if a thorough assessment of mediumistic communications were possible, mediums would be credited with much greater accuracy.

A milestone for me was reached one evening when the scheduled medium failed to turn up (a problem in Spiritualist churches due to the need to book mediums up to a year in advance), and "George", a local medium present in the congregation, was dragooned into doing the honours. This was one of those occasions when a substitute speaker surpassed the booked one! George was that rarity, a natural medium. He saw spirits as we see other people in the street, and had no problems with the clarity of his communications. I had, he asserted, a brother in spirit who had either died at birth or miscarried, and was therefore very close to me. Now, over the years I had received similar communications, but as I had only an elder sister, the communicator had always been identified as the son of an aunt who had died at a young age from TB. Delving deeper into the question of a miscarriage, I recalled my mother telling me that she had almost lost me in early pregnancy and had been forced to rest for a week or two. Further researches revealed that my mother's symptoms fitted a condition which was not medically recognised until several years after my birth. Many pregnancies, it was discovered were in fact twins, but usually one foetus was expelled at an early stage which often went unnoticed. Did

I have an unborn twin brother? It would indeed appear so, and it had taken sixty years before this was discovered. I had received numerous communications over the years which I had wrongly attributed.

It is evident from communications received that those in spirit take an interest in the progress of those in the body. They seem to be aware of particular problems of the moment and give timely advice. Many a time I have been given detailed descriptions of the manner in which a communicator passed which meant nothing to me, only to discover later that an acquaintance or family member was able to recognise them down to the last detail!

My involvement in Spiritualism uncovered an unknown world of circles which not only channelled wisdom from the Spirit World, but sometimes connected with other dimensions as well. We tend to think of the New Age movement as something separate from Spiritualism, but it came as a surprise to me to learn that Spiritualist circles also tune into Beings of Light and Ascended Masters, and there is a general consistency in what they receive. I was surprised to hear that circles often compared notes with each other about warnings of terrorist attacks, which sometimes turned out to be remarkably accurate. On one occasion a local medium felt she ought to pass on the warning to the police, and was subsequently contacted by two MI5 operatives and taken to a safe house in the locality for questioning. She was also able to help with the mystery of the death of another MI5 agent, who was thought to have been killed in an accident by confirming it was in fact murder. Subsequent to the interview, the agent concerned was at the London HQ when he saw the murdered agent at the end of a corridor.

Thinking the medium must have misled him, he called to the man, whereupon he turned and went into a room. Following him, the agent was astonished to find that the room was empty! A ghost at MI5 Headquarters, whatever next!

I was astonished to learn that the same medium had kept detailed records over the years during which her circle met which contained many correlations with the outpourings of New Age gurus about earth changes, raised consciousness and 2012. I had not realised the extent to which Spiritualism had advanced, but in retrospect it was entirely logical for sensitives to pick up the new spiritual energies which we are told are being directed at this planet. Now New Age gurus are generally treated with suspicion by the man in the street, with their colourful lifestyles and expensive seminars, but in the case of the medium in question we have an unassuming lady with no financial motive who is what might be termed a traditional Spiritualist, *and yet is telling us the same things as the New Age gurus!* For me, this is a strong indication that we should take more notice of the warnings we are being given about the immediate future, especially those contained within crop formations which are in the main free of human involvement. I go into more detail in chapter 6, but the point to be grasped is that Spiritualism has much to offer and it would be a mistake to dismiss it as merely providing evidence of the continuity of the human personality after death.

CHAPTER 11

CULTURAL DECEPTION

The title of this chapter is deservedly chosen because I consider that the modern western culture has been deliberately moulded by rather sinister forces with the intention of keeping the population in servitude, so that they serve the ends of the real rulers of this planet. Perhaps I had better explain myself, lest you imagine that I have strayed into the realms of conspiracy theories. I am and remain a parapyschologist. A parapsychologist studies the paranormal in a scientific manner and accepts only that which can reasonably be supported by the evidence, without resorting to speculation or supposition. This does of course mean that if "The powers that be" choose not to reveal what they know about the world of the paranormal (a racing certainty I would imagine!), then I am never going to know, unless I come by information from other sources which is likely to be anecdotal (of course some would point out that official information may in reality be disinformation, or misinformation released for some nefarious purpose, and therefore is not to be taken seriously either!). There is also the Official Secrets Act, and the need for a responsible researcher to keep within the law at all times. Conspiracy theorists do not feel any constraints and some display clear signs of mental instability. Whenever some major incident occurs, I wonder how long it will be before someone comes up with an alternative explanation to the "official" one, even though it may be quite clear from the initial reaction of the media what has really happened. In such people there is an automatic, psychological desire to fantasise about what *might* have happened and why the authorities might wish the public to think otherwise. Of course there is always the possibility that this might be the case, but the objective observer would require some evidence for a contrary viewpoint. Naturally conspiracy theorists had a field day over 9/11. I was earnestly assured by a good friend that it was not a plane but a missile in disguise which struck the Pentagon, and that the passengers on the real plane had been taken to a hangar and executed! When I politely asked what evidence she had to support this notion, she snapped "Well, that's obviously what must have happened" and declined to speak to me thereafter. One does not keep many friends for long in this business! I hope this will illustrate the difference between a parapsychologist and a conspiracy theorist, and why I stick to parapsychology.

Of course this does not mean that conspiracy theorists are always wrong. Given the nature of the world, there are bound to be some occasions when they get it right. One such was the death of Princess Diana. I said at the time that it would not be long before someone challenged the notion that a powerful car driven at high speed by someone who was drunk was very likely to suffer a fatal accident. The circumstances of the crash which killed Diana and Dodi are so well known and investigated in the minutest detail that they can admit of no dissent. The only slight area of doubt was the white car, still untraced, which is known to have struck the Princess' car a slight blow. This is indeed how an assassination would be carried out (nudge a car being driven by a drunken driver at high speed into a pillar), but given the chase which was taking place it is not inconceivable that other innocent vehicles might get caught up. One swallow does not make a summer! Thus it was that for several years I ignored the inevitable claims of the conspiracy theorists. That is, until one evening when I was chairing a meeting of APIS. I was astonished when a member asserted flatly that Diana had been murdered, since the person concerned was a well known sceptic for whom no evidence was ever enough. The remark was totally out of character. Asking him what evidence he had to support that assertion (the stock in trade of the parapsychologist!), I was rendered speechless by the calm response that a well known parapsychologist who occupied a key position in the media had telephoned him two days before the death of Diana to say that she would be murdered the coming weekend.

Lest you think that this was a bizarre coincidence, the call was prompted by an internal memo that was a guarded warning to news staff to prepare them for such an event. Because of the sensitive nature of this matter, I was unable to glean further details. I did suggest that the code of conduct required us to contact Mr Mohamed Al Fayed, but I was assured that he already knew the facts. My reaction to this revelation caused great amusement at the meeting but the point that struck me forcibly was that it was one of our more sceptical members who was asserting as fact something which went against his own attitudes and belief system regarding the paranormal. It met the key criterion that predictions have to be communicated to a third party *before* the event. An object lesson in how to assess claims of the paranormal if ever there was one!

CHAPTER 12

THE 2012 DEBACLE

Many writers pontificated on the meaning of 2012, indeed a weighty compendium of viewpoints was published but there were few definite predictions! Some writers elaborated on the Mayan calendar, others filled pages with flowery prose, and as a makeweight various authors enthused about an age of enlightenment within the current world paradigm, an unlikely scenario in my view since there is no obvious cause for this to happen. Until I had my NDEs in 2006, I took the view that the development of the 2012 scenario merited close monitoring. It was obvious that if a momentous event were to happen, it was unlikely to happen suddenly at a given moment. Rather, there would be a gradual build up over a long period. My tactic was therefore to assess the degree of awareness in society as a whole and the significance of world events. Clearly there had been an explosion in interest in what I call the Spiritual. A decade or so ago few people had ever heard of Reiki, now it is on offer in almost every High Street. Nor was there any discernible interest in angels outside of the churches; now we are bombarded with books on angelic beings and we even have Angelic Reiki. I had been fortunate in having a supply of cancer patients on which to practice, and therefore could measure new developments, energy shifts and the like in a clinical environment. Some patients did indeed notice and comment when, unknown to them, there had been an energy shift. Of course there was much "jumping on the bandwagon", and as with any new trend, there were plenty of people who saw it as a road to quick riches, but this does not detract from the validity of the shift in awareness.

Nor was this confined to spiritual aspects, for in the world of politics we have seen the collapse of Communism, and closer to home the uproar over the expenses claimed by MPs in the UK parliament. What the public was prepared to tolerate in the past, out of trust and ignorance, it is no longer prepared to accept. Some politicians have sought to capitalise on this shift in public opinion, in order to gain political power, but have our main political parties *really* changed? Time will tell, but I doubt if the fundamentals have altered. Pouring new wine into old wineskins will cause them to burst, and I believe that as the years progress we shall indeed see this happen in the form of social unrest, civil disobedience and a breakdown in the systems on which an ordered society relies. Given the undemocratic voting system we have in this country, which can return a government with a large working majority on as little as a third of the vote, a breakdown in law and order is a virtual certainty. We have already witnessed a collapse of the capitalist financial system. The consequences of this have yet to be fully realised, and too many are still living in a fools' paradise in which they see emergence from recession and a return to economic growth. Like many others I foolishly participated in the rush to benefit from the demutualization of the building societies, gaining greatly from inflated share values. Anyone rash enough to have predicted that all of the new banks would fail would have been laughed to derision, yet that is exactly what has happened and I have lost every penny of my new found wealth!

More subtle changes are also taking place behind the scenes. The Financial Services Authority (replaced in 2013 by two new regulatory bodies) has recently encouraged struggling building societies to give a stake in their business to large investors in order to keep afloat financially, but this means that investors in PIBS (Permanent Interest Bearing Shares) lose a proportionate share of their capital and income. Permanent indeed! And some of the nationalised banks have suspended payment of interest on PIBS! Who said no small investor would lose out? Despite the injection of vast sums of public money to prop up failed banks, the economy cannot recover because the banks have stopped lending in order to bolster their reserves with public money. With hindsight the banks should have been allowed to fail, and public money placed in a State bank which would have been able to inject cash into businesses in order to give impetus to the economy. But of course the status quo must be maintained to the financial detriment of the man in the street, because the world's top financiers are unwilling to lose their power, wealth and influence.

Now let us turn to the tricky subject of Earth Changes and weather events. Immediately we see the fear factor at work again. We are the cause of global warming, we are told, and a whole farrago of carbon credits and quotas are invented.

The end of the world is nigh unless we busy ourselves trying to reduce our carbon footprint. Once again we are being controlled by fear which is an unhealthy influence on us and prevents us from concentrating on spiritual matters. The fact of the matter is that global warming is cyclical, as history shows only too clearly, and archaeology proves that warming and cooling of the earth's atmosphere is probably as old as the earth itself. The scandal of manipulated data at the Climatic Research Unit at the University of East Anglia shows only too clearly how the public is being misled. The best educated guess as to the influence of human activities on global warming is that they contribute 0.9% to the percentage rise in overall temperatures. In fact, some authorities are suggesting that the peak of the warm cycle has now passed and we are actually entering a new Ice Age! Given the extreme winter weather in the northern hemisphere in the past few years, I can well believe it.

Looking at unusual weather events, it is true that we have seen quite a few in recent years. Hurricane Katrina devastated the city of New Orleans, the Asian tsunami killed a quarter of a million people, floods knocked out the water supply of thousands of people in the west of England, devastating earthquakes have hit Haiti and Chile, and a whole host of lesser disasters have occurred worldwide. My expectation is that such events will continue to occur, and this is the belief of many gifted seers.

As if the threat of weather events was not enough, we also have the threat of *solar* weather events. There have been suggestions that some of the ornate crop circle designs which appeared in the fields of Wiltshire in the summer of 2009 are warnings of solar flares or sunspots, which could cause havoc with our electrical systems and set us back to Victorian times. But even if they are, only major sunspots whose emissions are on a trajectory with earth are likely to affect us. Sunspots do occur, but they do not necessarily harm the earth, so indications of sunspot activity in crop circles may be only predictions, and not warnings. Again, only time will tell.

In the first draft of this book, written before 2012 (and the insolvency of the original publisher) I wrote the following:

"So what is going to happen in 2012? The problem with specific dates is not so much that nothing ever seems to happen, but that those who make predictions for specific dates rarely understand the significance of a particular date, and make unjustified assertions which of course are not usually fulfilled. So it is with the date of 21/12/2012. This is the end date of the current 26,000 year cycle of the Mayan calendar. What few people seem to realise is that whatever is going to happen will have happened by that date, and the changeover to a new state of consciousness will have taken place over a lengthy period before then. December 2012 marks the end of the change, not a sudden event."

Rather better than the predictions of most New Age gurus, wouldn't you agree?!

On the crucial date, 21/12/12, I decided against freezing to death and catching pneumonia on wet hilltops at Glastonbury, Stonehenge, Avebury and elsewhere, and meditated in my pyramid in an attempt to detect any new energies. When the world hadn't ended by lunchtime (surprise, surprise!), I abandoned my pyramid to catch up with my normal daily activities. Whilst I was right in that 21/12/12 marked the end of a very long period, I was perhaps a little unprepared for the full impact of the new energies. In the early part of January 2013 I suddenly found that I was overwhelmed by clients, most of them seeking to resolve longstanding health problems, get a new direction in life, or gain deeper spiritual awareness. If any proof was needed of the new energies (and I am one who always seeks proof), this was it. The stories related by the clients sometimes bore an uncanny similarity, almost as if they were reading from the same lifescript. The local Spiritualist church suddenly expanded its one page diary of events to four pages, adding events designed to aid the understanding of the new energies. Mediums briefed church members on likely consequences, some of which I must confess I found rather hard to believe, but as I have said before, only time will tell.

My miraculous recovery in 2006 and the revelations about the forthcoming transformation of human consciousness left me in no doubt about the reality of the changes which lie ahead. My experience was akin to the Rapture foretold in the New Testament. I had always believed that the Rapture would occur when it was least expected, but I also believed that the form it took would be beyond any human comprehension, and so it proved. The phraseology used in the Bible gives a reasonable impression of what actually took place in my own experience, although it is far removed from the belief of American evangelicals with bumper stickers warning that their cars may be driverless in the event of the Rapture! But can we expect anything else from so called Christians who bitterly opposed President Obama's plans to help the American poor who cannot afford health insurance? These folks are quite clearly not going anywhere, and I can foresee their anger and bewilderment when truly spiritual people become enlightened, while they are left behind! The terrible truth gradually dawned upon me that once the Rapture has occurred, the Return of Christ cannot be far behind!

In Christian eschatology there is much confusion about the doctrines of the Rapture and The Second Coming of Christ, so much so that the Church today rarely refers to them (in keeping with their refusal to expound on almost any point of doctrine, largely because the Church has just become a feel good alternative to the Sunday morning round of golf and nobody believes in anything anymore). If the Church were spiritually connected, they would of course be proclaiming the day of the Lord for all they are worth, but it seems likely that this event will pass them by, if only because traditional Christian belief requires a physical Return and the Resurrection of the Dead in a physical body. The Church lost the plot long, long ago and is now an impediment to spiritual progress. Once mankind has attained spiritual enlightenment it will quickly wither and die. It is quite clear now that the Second Coming of Christ will take the form of the indwelling of Christ's Spirit within the hearts of his followers (aka new spiritual energies). It is tragic that after some 2000 years of Christianity, few churchgoers will number among their ranks. How can sincere churchgoers receive Christ into their hearts when they oppose State healthcare for the poor (as the Bishops of the Church of England did in the UK), and vote for right wing political parties whose stance on the amassment of wealth and the care of the poor is the antithesis of everything Christ stood for? One does not have to be a theologian to see the hypocrisy of most Christians and where it will inevitably lead them.

I have already given my view on what is termed the Fall of Man (loss of spiritual awareness). I believe that what will happen will be the removal of the blockage in the brain of *Homo sapiens* so that he will once again recover the Paradise which has been lost. Man will recover his spiritual birthright and reconnect with the divine through the indwelling of the Christ spirit or energy. This is my interpretation of the doctrine of the Second Coming, and I believe it conforms fully with what the Bible says. The question which puzzles us most is the means by which it will happen. The Bible is quite clear: sound. The Universe was created by sound ("Word" in the book of Genesis means sound). The Bible says the Universe will change by the same means, when the Archangel blows the trumpet. Current theories as to how sound can change our molecular structure revolve around the reactivation of what is known as our junk DNA, which may be the key to spiritual awareness.

This conforms closely to what I was told in my first NDE. It sheds new light on what the Bible is trying to tell us. I am thrilled to think that we are on the verge of understanding the meaning of passages in the Bible which have vexed theologians for centuries. The pieces of the jigsaw are falling into place at long last, but what a tragedy it is that the Churches have largely given up and will miss the hour of glory.

Humanity has the opportunity for spiritual evolution, but how many will take it and what will happen to those who reject it. It has been said that an idea has to reach critical mass before it gains widespread acceptance, and some doubt that this could ever happen. But that view ignores the concept of physical changes induced by sound. All will have a choice, but many who are wedded to materialism and the concept of "beggar thy neighbour" will prefer to carry on with their present existence. The whole point, as was explained to me during my NDEs, is that WE ARE ALL GOD, and will have the opportunity to return to our true state of oneness with God. Those who reject this will have to remain in their unreformed state until, perhaps after repeated incarnations in other third dimensional worlds, they finally see the light. They will experience what the Bible aptly refers to as Hell, a state of separation from God.

Opinions differ about where the enlightened ones will go. Some say they will remain on earth and enjoy a Golden Age of peace and fulfilment. Others that they will ascend to divine realms (what the Bible calls Heaven). During my NDEs I was shown a vision of withered leaves (i.e. those who remain separated from God) being swept by the wind to end up being burnt in an incinerator. Not a pleasant prospect! There is a strong opinion that those unwilling to accept God will have to leave the planet for another dense, third dimensional realm. It has also been said that before the transformation process is complete, a majority of the earth's population will be culled by natural disasters, including famine and disease. Given that what is about to occur is outside the experience of any living being on this earth, and our Science is only just beginning to take the first faltering steps towards understanding the Universe and other realms, it is probably true to say that the mechanics of how this change will come about are beyond human comprehension, but of course once the capacity of our brains has been increased, we shall understand only too clearly! Lest you find this conclusion disappointing, console yourself with the thought that if we only had more time and scientists were far less egocentric, further advances in the field of quantum physics, astrophysics and sub atomic particles might well have provided a scientific answer to what is going to happen, and we would be much better prepared. The same could be said of the Churches if only they had not taken their eye off the ball. Whatever happens, and however it happens, it can only happen in accordance with natural law, whether that law is regarded as the operation of God's will or pure physics. Neither Church nor Science has met the challenge of providing us with a complete explanation of natural law, and ultimately both will have failed mankind.

CHAPTER 13

PREDICTIONS

I f the 2012 episode has taught us anything, it is that predictions relating to specific periods of time can almost always be safely ignored. Over the last forty or so years I have kept abreast of what was being predicted at the time, and in my view the number of fulfilled predictions is much less than could be accounted for by chance alone! At the time of writing (January 2013) it is being predicted that the global financial system will collapse in March, and remote viewers are said to be united in foreseeing widespread desolation of coastal areas following some kind of tsunami event in 2013—so you will be able to make your own judgement on the accuracy of these predictions! As with the ending of the Mayan calendar, a huge industry revolves around predictions in the form of books, lectures and conferences. Yet how many actually come to pass? Internet columnist George Ure (Texas, USA) regularly makes doomsday predictions about possible political and natural scenarios (often on Fridays, relating to the coming weekend!), but I cannot recall any which were actually fulfilled. Yet he carries on blithely in the same old way, and has a large following. The growth of the conspiracy theories movement in recent years has increased exponentially, and muddied the waters for parapsychologists looking for hard facts. I recall a leading conspiracy theorist talking to a devotee at a conference about a photo he was displaying which depicted the hijacked airliner hitting the twin towers in New York, and exclaiming that he could not understand why anyone could possibly believe that it showed a plane hitting a tall tower! My reaction was to mutter "Stop the world, I want to get off!". It is quite clear to me that conspiracy theories should be left to psychologists, who are well versed in dealing with those suffering from delusions. The problem for parapsychologists examining predictions is that many predictions emanate from conspiracy theorists and have no basis in fact.

There have been a few well respected seers down the ages, such as Edgar Cayce, and it is probably best to restrict any investigation to a detailed study of psychics with a proven track record. In my experience predictions relating to the near future tend to be more accurate than longer term predictions. Nevertheless when precise time frames are given they are often wide of the mark. This is explained as being due to the fact that time does not exist in other dimensions. In my view the question needs to be asked why predictions so rarely come to fruition, and this is where it gets interesting.

Recently it was announced that a group of scientists had secured funding to test their theory that the universe was really a computer simulation, and that we were merely players in some kind of cosmic computer game. Apparently they had devised a foolproof test! In the UK, researcher Anthony Peake is promoting his highly original theory that we are living out a recording, and claims to have discovered the function of certain types of brain cell which apparently can create the illusion of everything that we believe exists. This corresponds closely to what I was told in my NDE, and Anthony was greatly taken with my account of how I changed timelines and had to relive the day I died, which he felt lent weight to his theory. You will I am sure have grasped the implications of what this tells us about predictions. To take my case, a prediction that I would die in 2006 (which was actually conveyed to me by the angelic realm) could be said to have been fulfilled on my previous timeline, yet equally a prediction that I would survive would have been fulfilled on my new timeline!!!

If there are cosmic gamesters, each pitting their wits to ensure a successful outcome for "their" players against challenges generated by a supercomputer, then although it might be possible to have foreknowledge of the challenges, it would be impossible to predict the outcome which would depend on the skills of the gamesters! An example of this may perhaps be found in the solar flare of March 2012 which headed in the direction of the UK and mainland Europe. In the UK scientists had warned the Government of the likelihood of solar flares crippling the power supply system, and much media interest was generated by the announcement that one such flare was due to hit the UK in a few hours time. In fact nothing happened, the explanation being given out that when the flare reached us, the earth's magnetic field happened to be in the right magnetic state to repel the solar flare. Now, I am not sufficiently well versed in physics to know whether this explanation is true or not, but isn't this just the sort of last minute intervention a cosmic gamester would perform to prevent his players from experiencing a sudden breakdown of their civilisation?

One mystery about all this is why the Government, having been warned of the very real risk to the electrical system, did not shut down the National Grid (the UK's energy supply network)? Did they know it wasn't going to happen, and if so *how,* since scientists had determined there was a grave risk? Did they hesitate, or wasn't there simply enough time? If the latter, then it bodes ill for the future as next time (and there will be a next time) they might not get away with it. I suspect however, that the former is correct, because the *real* controlling power knows everything.

To date I have not come across anyone who has realised the significance of the March 2012 solar event. I hope this will encourage others to think laterally and read between the lines—there is a lot to be deduced by logical, rational thought, and if we don't spot these things, no-one else is going to tell us what they don't want us to know!

Perhaps I should end this chapter on a more positive note. It is worth recalling that a famous prediction of Nostradamus was that a great terror would come from the sky in the seventh month. The twin towers attack in New York took place in September, which in our calendar is the ninth month. But originally it was the seventh month, *septem* being the Latin for seven. In my book that is a prediction fulfilled!

In recent years I have been given several predictions about our moon. Now at school I was told that the moon was believed to have broken away from the earth at some distant stage in the past because physics told us that this was the most likely explanation. Some time later, after the USA had successfully reached the moon (yes, I really do believe that they did, since I was privileged to examine a sample of moon dust which had been entrusted to London University for research into its thermal properties), it was announced that the moon was now believed to have drifted from another galaxy and become caught by the earth's gravitational pull, as it did not have the same geological signature as earth. Yet the odds against this happening were such that chance alone could be virtually ruled out. Then, at the end of 2010, a Spiritualist medium of some repute locally predicted that early in the following year we would start to view the moon from a different angle. From my limited knowledge of astronomy I had thought that this was impossible without a change in the axis or orbit of either celestial body, and was astonished when the news soon broke on the internet that we could now see the moon from a different angle, illustrated by "before and after" pictures. Not only was this a prediction fulfilled, but it was one which had seemed scientifically impossible! Significantly the media remained silent on the matter, and the scientific explanation which I awaited eagerly was not forthcoming. The moon is known to have various effects on the earth (for example, tides), and I am left wondering whether there is a connection with the extreme weather and wide variations in the earth's magnetic field which we are currently experiencing?

I have also been told by a medium in a 21/12/12 briefing that we should watch the moon! Obviously his higher sources of information know something we don't! Another intriguing factor in all this is that we now know the moon is hollow, because when the lunar module landed it caused the moon to reverberate significantly for some time. So we have a planetary object which shouldn't be there, appears to change the angle from which we view it (which is intrinsically nonsensical), and is hollow, all of which contradict the laws of physics! I'll leave it there, but most people will be aware that a certain well known conspiracy theorist has gone a lot further!!

As I write the unexpected resignation of Pope Benedict XVI seems to have triggered the famous last pope, "Petrus Romanus" prediction of St Malachy. It is quite clear to me and a great many others that there is an underlying reason for this, and the current wave of paedophilia scandals swamping the Roman Catholic church gives a strong pointer. Here in the UK we have witnessed the unedifying spectacle of the most senior Roman Catholic cardinal in the land finally confessing to "inappropriate behaviour" with younger clergy, after lecturing us over a long period of time on the evils of homosexuality, even denying any personal involvement after being forced to resign by the Pope. This really does beggar belief! Yet the Roman Catholic church, knowing of the allegations, exalted him to the highest office as long as his victims maintained silence. How can anyone be deceived any longer by such a corrupt, unholy and hypocritical organisation? It is not my wish to upset anyone's religious beliefs, but surely the most devout Catholic must now face up to reality.

We now know that the last pope is an Argentinian, Jorge Mario Bergoglio, who hardly qualifies as Petrus Romanus, despite the tenuous links to the title promoted on the Internet, especially by the authors of a new book about the last pope! I imagine that, knowing of the Petrus Romanus prophecy, the conclave of cardinals in the Sistine chapel would have studiously avoided choosing anyone who could be linked with the prophecy. On the face of it, this would appear to be another failed prophecy, although Nostradamus' prediction of a black Pope around this time is of more interest, because Bergoglio is of the Jesuit Order, whose leader is termed "the black Pope". It will be even more interesting to see if another pope succeeds Bergoglio, as we can then put the prophecy of St Malachy finally to rest.

POSTSCRIPT

I finally put pen to paper after numerous communications, occurring over a long period at Spiritualist churches, had urged me to put pen to paper. I was granted a respite while this work was in preparation, but then I received warnings to be careful what I said, and I recalled the vow of secrecy imposed upon me during my NDEs. I believe that parapsychologists have a duty to behave responsibly and always keep in mind that uncorroborated channellings from entities of uncertain origin should never be taken at face value. Recently a purported alien communicator at a transfiguration séance assured the sitters that a fleet of alien spaceships was definitely on its way from a dying planet, seeking a sparsely populated area on earth to settle! I was quick to point out to the sitters that I had been listening to such warnings for fifty years and nothing of this nature had yet happened! The entity wanted a new circle to be set up to include myself, doubtless hoping that whatever line he wanted to promote might find its way into these pages. The Spiritualists decided the true identity of this entity was doubtful and declined to co-operate. As St Paul said, "test ye the spirits".

Perhaps I should say that I have no hidden agenda: this is an honest appraisal of a subject I have studied all my life. Yet I have to admit that I do have the benefit of personal experience, in particular the experience of what we term death, which opened up an undreamt-of dimension. Most of our current scientific and religious beliefs were shown to be almost entirely wrong. There is a vital "missing link" in our understanding of the Universe we live in, without which we cannot hope for full enlightenment. I count myself fortunate that I am one of a select band to have undergone an NDE which proved to be, for me at any rate, a mind bending and world shattering experience which provided the answer to many of the questions which have vexed mankind for centuries. In some respects I found the reality horrifying, and that is why these matters need to be treated with some care and discretion. For that reason I was sworn to secrecy.

I hope my intentions will be respected, for I believe that each must make up his own mind, and there are some who are not ready for such revelations. The discerning truthseeker whose curiosity has been aroused would do well to peruse the Background Information section which follows. If the concept I am hinting at seems simply unbelievable, then take some comfort from my own viewpoint, for most of my life, which was that such preposterous theories should be dismissed out of hand! Only the personal experience of meeting my maker (the lack of a capital M is deliberate) could change my view, but times are changing, and increasingly I am meeting enlightened souls who seem to know intuitively what I have spent a lifetime seeking. But surely that is as it should be, and bodes well for the future of mankind.

BACKGROUND INFORMATION

Therapies

www.shambhalahealingtools.com

www.angelicreiki.org

www.angeltherapy.com

www.dr**bradleynelson**.com/ Dr Nelson (USA) devised the Emotion Code which is founded on sound psychological principles

www.urtemadolphin.com An astonishing and highly spiritual lady who is a Breatharian (someone who lives without eating, an impossibility according to science)

and not forgetting . . . .

www.michaellewis.org.uk This details the services I offer in the field of parapsychology, especially healing. I am based in Barnet, on the borders of North London/Hertfordshire (UK). Emotion Code Therapy is available for patients who cannot travel using a proxy.

Magazines

More to Life Magazine: www.moretolifemag.co.uk

Flying Saucer Review: **www.fsr.org.uk**

Recommended Research Organisations (UK)

Anomalous Mind Management Contactee Helpline (AMMACH) :www.ammach.co.uk

Association for the Scientific Study of Anomalous Phenomena (ASSAP): www.assap.org

Wiltshire Crop Circle Study Group (WCCSG): www.wccsg.com

London Forum for the Study of Crop Circles and Other Mysteries (London Forum): www.londoncircles.net/

UFO's

www.slavespecies.com

www.amazon.co.uk/Gods-Eden-William-Bramley/dp/0380718073

www.solara.org.uk Solara An-Ra is a relative newcomer to the channelling scene. A gifted and most interesting lady who channels extraterrestrial beings and radiates spirituality

(It is also recommended that you read (or re-read) the book of Genesis and the Revelation of St John the Divine)

Crop Circles

www.thesiriusletters.com

www.cropcircleconnector.com

Make your charitable donations tax efficient! (UK only)

(some paranormal organisations are registered charities)

www.stewardship.org.uk

AUTHOR NOTES

Michael Lewis has had a lifelong interest in most aspects of the paranormal. He started off in the Society for Psychical Research (SPR) and later joined The Association for the Scientific Study of Anomalous Phenomena (ASSAP) He followed this with The British Unidentified Flying Object Research Association (BUFORA) and latterly the Centre for Crop Circle Studies (CCCS). He has spent countless cold nights in haunted properties up and down the country and investigated numerous reports of UFO sightings. He has taken an especial interest in crop circles because they fulfill many of the criteria for scientific study. In 2006 he underwent a series of Near Death Experiences (NDEs) which not only provided proof for many of his conclusions but greatly broadened his horizons. He now believes that very little of what we see and believe about the world around us is quite what it seems. Feeling that the best way of studying a phenomenon is to try and experience it himself, he has studied mediumship at Stansted College, the HQ of the Spiritualists National Union (SNU), with some modest success. More recently he trained as an AngelTherapist™ at Glastonbury under Doreen Virtue, and had some amazing experiences which convinced him of the reality of the angelic realms. The field of Healing has not been neglected, as Michael trained in Reiki 1 and 2 and latterly Angelic Reiki. He is not afraid to speak his mind, often to the horror of his scientific colleagues whom he feels will make little progress if they are hesitant to dip their toe into the water. He claims to be a born revolutionary and has never shirked controversy. His outside interests include the Liberal Democrats, and the railway preservation movement which is dear to his heart, having travelled extensively in his childhood over the East Anglian railway network in his youth, in the sight and sound of steam locomotives.

He insists he is not a Conspiracy Theorist, although he does concede that he has uncovered evidence that Princess Diana was murdered.